Challenges in the Theory and Practice of Play Therapy

Challenges in the Theory and Practice of Play Therapy provides an advanced and in-depth exploration of the issues and challenges relating to the training, theory and practice of child-centred play therapy. The ethos of the book is process orientated, and it discusses the particular therapeutic challenges that are encountered on a day-to-day basis.

Drawing upon clinical material and cutting-edge theory, David Le Vay and Elise Cuschieri bring together experienced practitioners from the field to explore key topics such as:

*   The therapeutic use of self within play therapy
*   Gender issues in play therapy
*   The play therapist's experience of self-doubt
*   Working with acquired brain injury
*   Working with developmental trauma
*   The role of research within play therapy
*   The role of experiential training groups in a play therapy training programme

Original and stimulating, *Challenges in the Theory and Practice of Play Therapy* will be of interest and value to all those working within the area of child mental health, both in practice and in training, and particularly those in the wider arts and play therapy community who are working therapeutically with troubled children.

David Le Vay is a qualified and accredited play therapist, dramatherapist and social worker. Since qualifying as a therapist in 1992, he has worked with children who have experienced significant loss, trauma and abuse, as well as with their families and carers. David has particular experience over the last 15 years of working with a service that provides therapeutic support for children and young people with sexually harmful and problematic behaviour. He is also a Senior Lecturer at the University of Roehampton on their MA Play Therapy programme and an approved BAPT play therapy supervis

Elise Cuschieri is a qualified teacher and   the
past 10 years, she has worked as a play thei   vice
with children and their families, pre- and   iior
Lecturer at the Uni   ...ay therapy programme. A   trainees.

Challenges in the Theory and Practice of Play Therapy

Edited by David Le Vay
and Elise Cuschieri

Routledge
Taylor & Francis Group

LONDON AND NEW YORK

First published 2016
by Routledge
2 Park Square, Milton Park, Abingdon, Oxon OX14 4RN

and by Routledge
711 Third Avenue, New York, NY 10017

Routledge is an imprint of the Taylor & Francis Group, an informa business

British Library Cataloguing in Publication Data
A catalogue record for this book is available from the British Library

Library of Congress Cataloging-in-Publication Data
Challenges in the theory and practice of play therapy / edited by
  David Le Vay and Elise Cuschieri.
    pages cm
  ISBN 978-0-415-73644-2 (hbk) — ISBN 978-0-415-73645-9 (pbk) —
  ISBN 978-1-315-67437-7 (ebk)
  1. Play therapy. I. Le Vay, David, editor. II. Cuschieri, Elise, editor.
  RJ505.P6C43 2016
  618.92'891653—dc23
  2015028341

ISBN: 978-0-415-73644-2 (hbk)
ISBN: 978-0-415-73645-9 (pbk)
ISBN: 978-1-315-67437-7 (ebk)

Typeset in Times New Roman
by Apex CoVantage, LLC
Printed in Great Britain by Ashford Colour Press Ltd

Contents

Foreword

Child-centred play therapy is a personal relationship in which the play therapist gives of herself or himself to the person of the child as fully as is possible in the immediacy of what is referred to as the relationship. This giving of self is a special gift upon which the play therapy relationship is built. It is not possible to adequately describe the facts of this relationship because words are inadequate to the task, or perhaps it is that my words seem so inadequate in attempting to describe what cannot be touched but is known in my mind and felt in my heart and soul. I find words terribly inadequate when I attempt to describe the kind of relationship that is experienced when I listen to understand the child rather than listening to answer, when I accept the child as she is without wishing she were different in some way, when I can be content with not knowing what I should be looking for, when I know without knowing that the child is capable of becoming so much more than has been described to me by significant adults in the child's life.

At this moment, I am aware that a part of me wants to lean back in my chair as thoughts race through my mind saying, "If you can't describe what you want to describe, then why go on?" Ah, but there is another part of me that says, "Perhaps my struggle will encourage some readers that this elusive dynamic referred to as the relationship is worth pursuing even though I cannot adequately describe its existence. Perhaps other readers will read and respond, 'Oh, I've been there, I've experienced that feeling also, but couldn't nail it down with words' and will be encouraged by my inadequacy." Therefore, I choose to trust that some individuals will be stimulated to think deeper thoughts as they read.

I think this must have been the purpose of the authors of the chapters in this book: to help the reader examine and reflect on seldom-examined facets of the play therapy relationship. In child-centred play therapy, it is, indeed, the relationship that is therapeutic, and the person of the therapist is more important than anything the therapist knows how to do. I want to become so absorbed in the relationship with the child that everything I do becomes a response to the relationship. Everything that is important in play therapy happens within the context of the relationship, and everything that happens in play therapy impacts the relationship.

This is a book that encourages openness by living out openness and vulnerability on the pages of the chapters. In Chapter 1, David shares his struggle to "untangle some of the conceptual knots in the concept of the use of self within child-centred play therapy" and his experience that they are "complex and hard to unravel." Yes, attempting to describe the play therapist's use of self in the relationship is difficult, because there is no prescribed identifiable role for the child-centred play therapist to be a certain way. Use of self is a way of being rather than a way of doing. The child-centred play therapy relationship is not an experience in which the therapist assumes a certain role or tries to do things in a prescribed manner. That would not be real or genuine. When I have immersed myself in the immediacy of the relationship with a child, it is not possible for me to think about being a certain way, doing a certain thing, or plan what I think should be done next. This is a way of living life with a child moment by moment, not a technique to be applied when it seems to be needed. What I am trying to describe is a way of being with a child that is devoid of planning or predetermined structure, a relationship in which the play therapist has no expectations of the child, a relationship in which the child feels safe, safe enough to express and explore whatever wells up in her, a place where she can just be her "own little ol' self" on her terms without being concerned about meeting someone else's expectations, a place of understanding and acceptance, a place where she can discover unknown and unused strengths, a place where she is prized as a person of worth, a healing relationship.

A beginning play therapist I was supervising described her discovery of this process as:

> Through experiencing children in play therapy, I have come to understand the living nature of the therapeutic relationship. I more fully understand and feel the dynamic experience of encountering a child, finding in the child what I can never discover in textbooks – myself in action with the child. I needed to move beyond intellectual descriptions and classification, beyond the abstract view of helping, and to encounter my own inner experience. It is not easy to be in intense relationships with a child.

I'm glad Elise persevered in being intentional about her own process of self-discovery when self-doubts about writing Chapter 2 of this book plunged her into feeling "Perhaps this is the end of the road" and "I couldn't carry on." In her struggle to allow the process to unfold, she discovered that being a play therapist and a writer are both a process of becoming rather than an event.

As I have written in my book *Play Therapy: The Art of the Relationship*, attainment of personality characteristics that facilitate the play therapy process and development of the relationship are not nearly as important as the continual, self-motivating, never-ending process of striving to attain and incorporate these dimensions into one's life and relationships with children. It is the play therapist's intentionality in this striving that is the dynamic therapeutic facilitative quality in the process, not the attainment of describable dimensions. Intentionality defies description.

Another graduate student I was supervising in play therapy described the freeing aspect of self-understanding and self-acceptance this way:

> The more I understand myself and admit to being imperfect, the more I can let go of self-consciousness and the need to fulfill a role expectation of being a therapist. This preconceived image has deprived me of the freedom and spontaneity through which my best strengths may be developed. I no longer feel in the playroom that I am performing a stressful chore, but constructing a personally creative encounter with a child. I am discovering that when I am uptight it is difficult to approach another person, and that with increased relaxation I can see myself in action, to note the false moves or the extra steps I have unconsciously incorporated into my behavior. My goal is to project a personal self as fully as possible. This in turn facilitates the movement of the child toward becoming the self he is in the developing relationship. The more I am able to appreciate my own uniqueness, the more able I will be to accept the uniqueness of the child I am with in the play therapy relationship.

Perhaps this was written for Elise, David and Jan in Chapter 6.

Garry L. Landreth
Regents Professor Emeritus
Department of Counseling
University of North Texas

Preface

The idea for this book grew gradually from the cumulative momentum of unfinished snatches of conversation across our cluttered desks high up in the windy heights of our shared attic office at the University of Roehampton. Between noisy bouts of banging, thumping pipes caused by perennial heating problems and the appearance of ever-resourceful squirrels that sneak in through the windows to make away with our lunch, the two of us would talk about the shared dilemmas, challenges, practice and training issues that arose both through our own respective clinical work as practising play therapists and through the recurring issues that seem to come up as we accompany our students through their intense, 2-year play therapy training.

As said, our conversations have generally been accompanied by the discordant background sound of the office heating, sometimes just a gentle, rather hypnotic knocking and sometimes a banging so violent it sounds as if the whole building is about to collapse around us. Often, the sound is reminiscent of the engine room of some great transatlantic ocean liner. We have learned over time that the only way to regulate the noise and moderate its level of intrusiveness is through a rather hit-and-miss approach of adjusting the temperature of the various radiators both within our office and in the surrounding corridors. Sometimes we have to turn them all up to high, which means that the room gets very hot and we have to open the windows . . . which means that the squirrels get in. Sometimes we have to turn them all off, which leaves us feeling too cold. But more often than not, it is a process of fine tuning as we seek just the right degree of pressure in the system to achieve a degree of balance and, hopefully, blissful silence.

And so the querulous radiators and temperamental pipes have become something of a background motif for our formative discussions about this book, something about flow, adjustment, temperature, regulation, proximity and a constant striving to find the optimal point of *being*. It is the relationship among the various parts of this system that needs attending to in order to achieve a point of balance and equilibrium, symbolic, perhaps, of some of the challenges inherent within the process of child-centred play therapy. As play therapists, we need at all times to attend to the relationship and provide the core, attitudinal conditions that enable the child to play creatively and imaginatively as well as being mindful of our own internal noise, the discordant reverberations of incongruence as we seek to balance our own feelings of uncertainty and anxiety.

And so this book, *Challenges in the Theory and Practice of Play Therapy*, brings together a number of experienced child-centred play therapists who explore some of the specific challenges that are encountered on a day-to-day basis, challenges that are perhaps not always talked about openly or explored fully. Some of these challenges relate to therapist-directed, process-oriented issues such as the therapeutic use of self and how we strive to remain congruent and authentic in our work whilst managing some of the tensions around self-disclosure. Connected with this is the ubiquitous challenge of therapist self-doubt and the critical inner voice that often accompanies us into the playroom. Further chapters explore some of the wider systemic and societal challenges that might impact our work as play therapists, namely those of gender and culture and the need to be mindful of how these dynamics might get played out within our work with both children and families. Other challenges explored relate to the demands of working with children who have very specific needs, for example, those with acquired brain injury or children who have experienced developmental trauma and are presenting with stuck, traumatic play. And of course there is the role of research: how we seek to understand and evaluate the therapeutic value of what is actually happening in the playroom. Finally, we spend some time reflecting upon issues of play therapy training and specifically the role of the 'process group' within a play therapy programme and the extent to which this experience contributes to the trainee's developing sense of self-awareness.

We do not seek to necessarily provide answers in this book but rather highlight the questions as we explore some of the less travelled paths of child-centred play therapy. It is not a book about techniques or tools; it is a book about being – not doing. We wondered who this book might be for, who might read it. Would it be an advanced text for qualified, experienced play therapists or a book that might be helpful for trainees and newly qualified therapists as they embark on their newfound careers? Ultimately, it is what it is, and people will make of it what they will. But in essence, throughout our own writing and that of our fellow contributors, we have sought to hold onto process rather than outcome; that in the end it is about what happens in the playroom and, ultimately, how we understand what it is that is happening.

David and Elise
Roehampton
March 2015

Most of the chapters that follow draw on clinical material from the authors' clinical play therapy practice. Names and details have been changed in order to anonymise the cases and to protect the identities of the children involved. Nevertheless, we are aware that in the course of reading this book, you may think you recognise a particular case described. If that is so, we hope the vignettes/case depictions are read in the spirit they were written – with utmost respect for the children and their families described and as a way of increasing knowledge and understanding about the unique process of child-centred play therapy. Thank you.

Chapter 1

To be or not to be?

The therapeutic use of self within child-centred play therapy

David Le Vay

The Rogerian principle of congruence is rightly understood as being a fundamental core condition of the play therapy process. Similarly, we talk about the concepts of genuineness and authenticity in our practice, indeed not simply concepts but ways of being that lie at the very heart of what it means to be a child-centred play therapist. But experience suggests that many play therapists still grapple with the idea of what it means to be truly congruent and whether to hold such a position is ever really viable or indeed desirable and hence the therapist filter that we seek to apply as a way of managing the complex relational ebb and flow between self and other. Clearly, the nature of this personal filter is shaped by experience, training and developing self-awareness: the learned intuitive state of unconscious competence perhaps, as well as the particular, unique quality of the therapeutic relationship.

The Rogerian approach holds that the personhood of the therapist is the central element of the change process; but what do we mean by personhood, and how does this relate to the therapeutic use of self? Certainly, there are degrees of personal transparency and opaqueness, the extent to which we make ourselves truly present and visible to the child, but transparency is not the same as congruence, just as congruence is not the same as self-disclosure or indeed personhood as the use of self. The relationship between these concepts often seems complex and unclear, assumed perhaps rather than understood. So what do we mean by *use of self* and how does this inform the desired attitudinal states of congruency and authenticity? How, as therapists, do we make decisions about self-disclosure and what we choose to share or withhold? In this chapter I aim to explore some of these perennial questions and practice challenges faced by the play therapist, the extent to which we bring ourselves into the work that we do and, ultimately, into our relationships with the children that we are working with therapeutically.

In terms of personal process, I have experienced writing this chapter as something of a challenge, the concept of the use of self within child-centred play therapy (CCPT) being complex and hard to unravel. As play therapists, we talk liberally about notions of congruence, authenticity, genuineness and transparency, all of which contribute to that which we might generically refer to as the use of self. Along with empathy and unconditional positive regard (UPR), these are understood as being the essential, attitudinal pre-conditions of CCPT, conditions that need to be both felt internally and expressed externally in order to facilitate a positive therapeutic experience for the child. But there is an intangible, subjective and ultimately indefinable quality to these therapeutic conditions that does not easily lend itself to a process of measurement or evaluation. So in an attempt to untangle some of these conceptual knots, I will begin by seeking some understanding of the term *use of self* and then look at the notions of personhood, congruence and self-disclosure as they might apply to play therapy before going on to explore some of the more specific practice issues that invariably arise as we bring ourselves into our work with children. Throughout this chapter I will be drawing upon brief clinical vignettes from my practice, identifying details from which have been disguised and anonymised in order to maintain confidentiality.

Use of self

There are, I would suggest, connections between the use of self and the feelings of therapist competence and self-doubt that have been discussed elsewhere in this book and how confident we are in the personal and professional identity of ourselves as therapists. To use ourselves in our work, to use the *self* as an agent of change, requires by definition a confidence and knowledge in who we are. As Rogers said, "to be a fully authentic therapist . . . you have to feel entirely secure as a person. This allows you to let go of yourself, knowing confidently that you can come back" (Baldwin, 2000: 36). But sometimes perhaps we lose our way, lose sight of our professional identity as a therapist or become pulled out of shape by either the clinical, interrelationship dynamics of the therapy itself or perhaps by external events that impact who and how we are in the playroom at any given moment. Indeed, what is it that either empowers or disempowers our capacity to let go and find our way back?

The pathway is not always clearly signposted, the route not always apparent. Yes, we have markers along the way, weathered cairns of knowledge, experience and training. Sometimes eroded by familiarity, these metaphorical stone markers give a contextual sense of the landscape and the shape and contours of the surrounding environment, a relief map one might say. But often as therapists it is in the absence of such markers that we are required to have faith in the process and to trust that we are heading in the right direction, and how we use ourselves and bring our own self-awareness into the therapeutic relationship is ultimately the most important and uniquely significant element of this process. As Landreth (1991: 65) says, it is about being real – a "living out of the self in the moment of the relationship" – but for both trainees and experienced therapists the challenge is often in knowing how real to be. To be or not to be? For trainee play therapists especially this question can evoke some powerfully conflictual and often paralysing responses as they begin to feel their way through the uncharted territory of the therapeutic process. After all, there are some inherently paradoxical tensions between the juxtaposed positions of authenticity and self-withholding that tend to be communicated to trainees. In a sense, the ambiguous message conveyed is 'to be but don't be' – something of an existential double bind, one might suggest.

But it strikes me that the term *use of self* is something of a misnomer in the context of CCPT. It is perhaps not so much about how we *use* ourselves in our work, the suggestion being of some kind of conscious, active application of the self as a therapeutic tool, but more an acknowledgment that our personhood, our very presence, pervades, permeates and diffuses through the therapeutic relationship at all times, for better or worse. As the saying goes, 'wherever I go, there I am', and the notion that we can leave ourselves outside the playroom and enter the session "without memory or desire" (Bion, 1970) just as we might hang up our coat is, I would suggest, more of an aspiration than a reality.

Lanyado (2004) talks about the *presence* of the therapist, and in many ways this is a more helpful way to think about the use of self, the emphasis more upon being than doing as we consider the dynamic, interpersonal nature of the relationship between ourselves and our clients. As Lanyado suggests, it is perhaps easier for us as therapists to think about what does not (or should not) come into the therapy room with us than to think about what actually does. Clearly, we all endeavour to put aside whatever personal issues, opinions, thoughts, feelings, attitudes that we might be experiencing prior to entering the playroom with a child, to hit the internal 'restore to factory settings' switch that helps us to re-set ourselves between sessions. To think about what we bring in with us, that which slips under the radar of our personal consciousness, inevitably requires us to acknowledge our fallibilities, our growing edges, our blind spots: those aspects of ourselves of which we may not be so consciously aware but nevertheless seep osmotically across the therapeutic boundary between self and other. As Lanyado says, "the need for the therapist to continue to scrutinise his or her inner world, to sift the impact of the (child) from the background noise of the therapist's personal domain, remains throughout the therapist's working life" (2004: 4).

So perhaps it is not so much what we should leave by the door but an awareness of what it is we are actually taking through with us. Let us not aspire to hanging up our identity along with our hat and coat but acknowledge and accept who we are and the unique quality this brings to the therapeutic process. We cannot separate self and other, nor should we, and the conceptual frame of the opaque, analytical mirror does not sit comfortably with CCPT. If play therapy is about a way of being and all that this entails, then we cannot deny who we are and need to accept that we are all unique individuals who will work in our own unique, individual way. Sometimes this means taking risks; as Landreth suggests, "allowing one's self to be vulnerable enough to be impacted or touched emotionally by the child's experiences and feelings requires personal courage and an openness to risk sharing self in a very personal way that is non-defensive" (Landreth, 1991: 92). This does not mean a sharing of self in the form of self-disclosure but in the sense of having sufficient self-awareness and understanding to allow us to respond intuitively to the child's creative and expressive communication. This requires being open to our vulnerabilities, our mistakes and misjudgements (as well, of course, as our strengths) and whilst we all clearly aspire to being as good a therapist as we can, we also have to accept that the process of learning never stops – and if it does it is perhaps time to stop being a therapist. Being human is a developmental experience, as is being a therapist, and I strongly eschew ideas of perfection or expertise. Once someone has declared themselves an expert, I would suggest they have little left to learn, and that is a position I would personally view with some caution.

The personhood of the play therapist: Congruence and authenticity

Personhood within a child-centred play therapy context can be thought about as the very essence of what it means to be fully present in the playroom. It is about being congruent, authentic and genuine and at all times open to the immediacy of our feelings and experiences. It is also about recognising and accepting who we are, the individual and unique set of qualities, traits and characteristics that make up our *self* and how these become manifest within the relationship with the child. Landreth talks about the quality of *being there* for the child – "the play therapist knows that being present with the child requires much more than a physical presence; that being there is truly an art form that makes the play therapy experience unique for the child" (1991: 90). Personhood then is about *therapeutic presence*, about being there in body, in thought and in feeling; an overarching expression of self and experience that encompasses and communicates the core conditions of child-centred play therapy: congruence, empathy and unconditional positive regard.

For the purposes of this discussion, I will focus mainly upon the core condition of congruence, the expression of self or personhood that connects most strongly to our sense of therapeutic presence in the playroom. Clearly, empathy and UPR are themselves expressions of congruence; they are all part of the felt, attitudinal *way of being* spoken of earlier, and it is hard to disentangle one from the other; congruence being the means through which empathy and UPR are conveyed. By way of defining congruence, Rogers says:

> Whatever feeling or attitude I am experiencing would be matched by my awareness of that attitude. When this is true, then I am a unified or integrated person in that moment, and hence I can be whatever I deeply *am* . . . when self-experiences are accurately symbolised, and are included in the self-concept in this accurately symbolised form, then the state is one of congruence of self and experience.
>
> (1959: 206)

A state of congruence then would suggest that the therapist's external expressions of self are matched or in harmony with their felt, internal experience, an integration of thought, awareness and affect that together create a sense of authenticity. Of course, this does not mean that every thought or feeling is communicated explicitly to the child. At various times we might experience feelings of irritation, boredom, anger, rejection or excitement, but to express these feelings indiscriminately to the child would clearly be both inappropriate and irresponsible (and certainly not therapeutic), and in this sense the distinction between transparency and congruence can begin to be made. As Means and Thorne (2000) have cautioned, congruence should not be viewed as an invitation for the play therapist to communicate to the child any and every thought or feeling that may arise. Congruence then is not about allowing the child to know or see all of one's internal process but instead to have sufficient self-awareness and insight and understanding to know what should be expressed or withheld, child directed or self directed, with the aim being always to enhance the therapeutic relationship. Realness is "being aware of and accepting one's own feelings and reactions with insight into the accompanying motivation and being willing to be oneself and to express these feelings and reactions when appropriate" (Landreth, 1991: 65).

Being self-aware also requires us to reflect upon how we communicate on a non-verbal, bodily level. Irritation with a child can be communicated through a momentary look in the eye, a furtive glance at the clock, tone of voice or posture and movement. Congruence, then, is communicated both verbally and non-verbally and is ultimately the felt, authentic experience of being in the presence of another. The children that we work with, especially children who have experienced trauma and abuse, are intuitively, vigilantly aware of body language and non-verbal communication; it is after all a part of their protective coping strategies, and I would suggest that most children have an instinctive sense of the extent to which an adult is being authentic or otherwise. The façade or mask of incongruence, wherein there is a divergence or discrepancy between the internal experience of the therapist and the externally communicated self will, I suggest, be all too apparent to the child in the playroom.

The significance of non-verbal communication should not be under-estimated. Barrett-Lennard (1962), who developed the Relationship Inventory (BLRI) as a means of assessing the core conditions of person-centred therapy, found that whilst congruent therapists are more honest, direct and sincere in their communications than are therapists of other theoretical disciplines, incongruence is "most often demonstrated through inconsistencies between what therapists say and what they imply through gestures, expressions or tone of voice and through indications of anxiety, discomfort or tension" (Ray, Jayne and Stulmaker, 2014: 19). Emphasising this point, Van Fleet, Sywulak, Sniscak and Guerney (2010) stated that a key element of the attitudinal state of congruence is the consistency among body language, intonation and the spoken words of the therapist. In this sense, it is as much about how we communicate as it is about what we are communicating.

Of course congruence, genuineness or authenticity as a desired state of being with a child is not always easy or comfortable. At times we may feel deeply conflicted or feel challenged by the child who tests the boundaries of therapy and pushes at our personal limits of acceptance. Some children we may naturally warm to, others less so. Some will evoke powerful feelings of rage, disgust or idealisation. There is a visceral vitality and directness to working with children therapeutically, communicated through the dynamic quality of their dramatic play, and to truly *be* with a child means by definition to open oneself up to the powerful and often intense projective and transferential material that is so much a part of the therapeutic relationship. During the course of my work with very traumatised children I can recall many times that feeling of anxious anticipation as I awaited the tellingly urgent ring of the clinic's doorbell, knowing that it was going to be another long, hard session that would test my capacity to emotionally contain the child. Is it always possible to be truly congruent? Certainly, there have been times when I have been aware of my own façade, the act of projecting an external sense of containing calmness and acceptance when internally I have been working hard to manage my own anxiety. At times like these one needs to be self-aware enough to monitor these feelings of incongruity, accept them and ensure that they don't intrude upon the therapeutic process. A little self-talk or the faithful internal supervisor is always helpful at these moments. A state of congruence then perhaps needs to be viewed as an aspiration, a therapeutic way of being that we would all strive for in our work with children whilst recognising that there are times when this does not always feel attainable. As Ray, Jayne and Stulmaker (2014) suggest, congruence is experienced as a flow within the relationship between self and other – between play therapist and child, a continuum along which the therapist endeavours to reach an optimum state of authenticity.

Self-disclosure

I recall once working with a young adolescent, I'll call him Shane, who had experienced a catalogue of trauma and abuse throughout his childhood. Perched precariously on the edge of his chair, coat tightly wrapped around him and hood pulled down over his eyes, this was a young person deeply affected by intense feelings of anxiety, mistrust and shame. Our first session together was pervaded by his deeply withholding silence, broken only by the uncomfortable sound of him methodically cracking his knuckles. I remember feeling quite helpless in the face of his intense anxiety, my words feeling like bullets that could pierce his fragile, protective shell. His threat responses were highly aroused, his body tensed in readiness to either fight or run. Conscious of not wanting to allow my own anxiety to drive my responses, I simply reflected upon what was happening in the present; the sound of his cracking knuckles, how this made me feel physically and wondering aloud about whether his actions might hurt or harm him.

From under his hood and baseball cap, Shane told me that he did not feel pain – that nothing ever hurt him – and he went on to crack the joints of his wrists, ankles and even neck, clearly enjoying my own rather pained, winced responses to his bone-cracking exploits. Somehow, we started talking about escapologists and the notion of being double-jointed, which led us further into a conversation about the numerous accidents and injuries Shane had experienced over the years. Metaphorically, the sub-text to this exchange seemed to be about his experience of developmental trauma, the feelings being held and communicated on a bodily level, letting me know how much in fact he had been hurt despite his claim to be impervious to pain. He then showed me various scars on his legs and arms that had been caused by all manner of jumping, climbing and falling over the course of his childhood. I had some small scars and marks on my lower arm, and for some reason I found myself showing these to Shane, and together we joked about the scene from the film *Jaws* in which Richard Dreyfuss and Robert Shaw compared their respective scars and injuries as they sailed out to sea to do battle with the great white shark (interestingly, sharks became a theme of Shane's later sessions). Later on, I reflected upon this moment and wondered why I had decided upon this act of self-disclosure. Was it a boundary transgression? Had I allowed my own sense of personal boundaries to become pulled out of shape as a consequence of some unconscious dynamic? On reflection, I feel it was perhaps an intuitive use of self, that in the present moment of the session I was seeking a way in which to connect with Shane, a point at which I could momentarily join him in his story and find a way of being together through a shared metaphor.

Wosket (1999) defines the use of self as something that involves the "operationalisation of personal characteristics so that they impact upon the client in such a way as to become potentially significant determinants of the therapeutic process" (1999: 11). One might think of this then in the context of an intervention, with the aim of enhancing or facilitating the therapeutic process in some way, although this suggests some degree of intentionality, which may not always be the case, just as the outcome may not always be positive. In the case example of Shane, my explicit use of self (in this case in the form of self-disclosure) did indeed help facilitate the therapeutic process to the extent that it opened up a rich dialogue in which we found a shared metaphor to be able to begin to explore his experience of abuse and hurt. It can feel a risk at times, but a risk that involved some degree of clinical rationale. But there have also been many times where my use of self, intentional or otherwise, has been unhelpful, mistaken or ill considered. The dynamic immediacy of the play therapy encounter invariably means that the therapist is only ever in partial, conscious control of the process of self-disclosure.

As said, we reveal ourselves (or give ourselves away) each time we sit in a consulting room with a parent or with a child in the playroom. The way we sit, our tone of voice, eye contact, posture, body language, how we walk and talk, the clothes we wear, the presence or absence of a ring on our finger. We disclose information about ourselves at each and every moment of our interaction. Paint marks on our hands suggest the earlier presence of another child. A pregnant play therapist is disclosing not only that she is going to have a child and become a mother but also that she has had sex. All these facets of ourselves, revealed both consciously and unconsciously, will inevitably impact the dynamic of the relationship and evoke deep feelings within the child of curiosity, jealousy, idealisation or destructive envy as they realise that their therapist does indeed exist outside the playroom.

Recently in a session, a young boy asked me if I had a son. My first instinct was to simply give a direct answer, the voice in my head saying, 'for goodness sake, just tell him what he wants to know'. I found myself stalling as I sought to understand the meaning of his question. The boy had been placed with foster carers soon after his birth and had seen his father just once or twice since that time and not for many years. Earlier in the session he had spontaneously mentioned his father and seemingly surprised himself in the process, telling me it was strange, as he never usually thinks about him. From a transference/counter-transference perspective, it felt clear that the therapeutic relationship had aroused some sense of paternal feeling or association. His question, to my mind, was on one level a simple desire to know if I was a father but on another a poignant, felt expression of paternal absence, a feeling that perhaps had become tangibly crystallised within the intimacy of the play therapy space, the idealised sub-text to the question perhaps being 'can you be my father?' This was what I sought to reflect in response to his question: that it felt like he was thinking a lot about his father today and about what it would be like to have a 'dad' available for him. He was persistent. 'So do you then . . . have a son?' Again, I acknowledged his strong desire to know about me, that he wanted reassurance that he had me all to himself for the sessions but in the face of his continual persistence had to invoke the 'emergency clause' and explain that play therapists do not usually talk about their own families to children. As ever, it felt an unsatisfactory response, not quite punitive but something of a therapeutic put-down, and it is moments like these that can crystallise the therapeutic tension that can sometimes occur between congruence and withholding.

But the issue, in the context of this discussion, is what would have been the impact or consequence of disclosing this personal information, and would it have helped or hindered the therapeutic process? My experience is that this kind of personal self-disclosure is rarely helpful. The focus/emphasis of the session would have shifted away from the child and onto myself and led him to become preoccupied with my own family story. And to have disclosed whether I had a son (to a boy who is struggling with the absence of his own father) would have paved the way for all manner of projective fantasies, idealisation, jealousy and envy that may have clouded or obscured the process of therapy. Indeed, my own initial wish to answer the question honestly and directly (rationalised through the earnest desire to be authentic and congruent) may well have stemmed from my personal counter-transference response to this boy; the fact being that I do not have a son and to have answered as such might have been more about indulging my own unconscious paternal fantasies. It is always interesting when personal boundaries become distorted or pulled out of shape and says much, I think, for the power of the unconscious dynamics at play.

Interestingly, in his subsequent session the boy announced that he had been thinking about conducting some scientific experiments and wanted to try and splice together some DNA from various creatures to see what kind of animal he might end up with, adding that by using a drop of his own blood he could include himself in this experiment. Holding in mind last week's exchange I wondered about the questions he might have about his own genetic makeup and the kind of DNA from which he was created. His quest for scientific discovery was perhaps more about a search for his own identity and how he made sense of his place in the world, and we talked about this for a while, about the idea of being 'part mum and part dad'. But again I wondered about the possible sub-text to his 'experiments'. Was he expressing a desire to splice the two of us together, a ritualistic sharing of DNA wherein I would become his long-yearned-for father? The strong paternalistic response this boy evoked within me did, I think, communicate something about the tangibly acute sense of loss he felt in relation to his own father and in this context I was glad that I had indeed held the line the previous week.

But the immediacy of these exchanges is always a challenge. Another time, I recall working with a boy on the autistic spectrum whose father had died when he was a young child. During the course of one session he said to me, ". . . well you're old, so your dad's probably dead as well isn't he?" For some reason I did answer him directly – "yes, my dad is dead too . . . just like yours", and in my defence I think the directness of my self-disclosure was partly in response to the literal quality of this boy's ASD (autism spectrum disorder) alongside my sense that I did not think this disclosure would impact negatively upon the therapeutic process, or may in fact be helpful. Whether it was or not, I am not sure.

So decisions around verbal self-disclosure can on one level be thought about in the context of a continuum between the personal and the impersonal and the degree to which the information will either enhance or hinder the therapeutic relationship – in other words, disclosure as a form on therapeutic intervention. If a child asks if I am married or have children I am generally very clear that this is information not to be disclosed whilst acknowledging the child's desire to know and the underlying meaning of the question. If a child asks what kind of car I have, what I had for breakfast or what football team I support, I may or may not answer depending upon the nature of our relationship and whether I feel to answer the question directly will be beneficial to the relationship; or indeed if it doesn't matter. There are times when a clear, unambiguous response to a question can be just what the child needs.

I have also experienced many interesting sessions with children and young people talking about films we have seen or books that we have read, shared stories that have been helpful in exploring themes in the session or an understanding about a child's personal narrative identity. For example, I recall a young person who was very pre-occupied by labyrinths and mazes, images of which would often appear within his drawing and paintings during the session. I shared with him the story of Theseus and the Minotaur and how Theseus was able to find his way back through the labyrinth after defeating the Minotaur with the help of Ariadne's thread. The story connected strongly with his experience of trauma and fear of becoming disconnected or lost, and in this sense the symbolism of the thread was particularly helpful. Clearly, this form of intervention involves a level of personal sharing but can be very valuable when one has a clear therapeutic goal in mind.

I am also greatly indebted to my childhood obsession with Marvel comics, now that they have been cinematically realised and brought into the collective consciousness of a new generation of children. They are metaphorical gold dust to the play therapist, but on several occasions I have caught myself talking to children about the 'Marvel Universe' more as a way of indulging my own fanciful whims than with any particular therapeutic aim in mind. Activities like Winnicott's 'squiggle game', which I often use in my sessions, similarly demand some aspect of the use of self, but it is the very relational, reciprocal quality of these kinds of activities that make them so valuable as a form of engagement. I am also a keen advocate of having games like Jenga and Connect4 in the playroom, relational games which of course demand the use of self to varying degrees.

But as said, self-disclosure (in relation to use of self) needs to be thought about in much broader terms than just that revealed of a personal nature. Wosket (1999) talks about the notion of *relational self-disclosure*, the felt-sense of the therapist making themselves tangibly visible within the therapeutic relationship. As Wosket says,

> This type of self-disclosure arises from my felt responses within the relationship with the client. These may be thoughts, feelings, images, fantasies, echoes or resonances, bodily sensations, lapses or increases in energy that can normally be trusted as having some relevance and significance because they arise from the meeting between us and not from something I choose to bring to the meeting.
>
> (1999: 52)

Relational self-disclosure then is about being manifestly present within the relationship, allowing those felt-responses to come into the session with the aim, as Wosket says, of achieving a greater degree of reflexivity within the relationship; the relational ebb and flow of developing knowledge and awareness.

Wosket talks about the 'edge of awareness', that point at which the therapist reaches "beyond conscious competence to aspects of yet unfathomed capability, where new possibilities of working are forming only in that precise moment of being with a client" (1999: 30). Within the play therapy process children are occupying that very same territory, the hinterland between the conscious and unconscious – the symbolic and the concrete – and it can be a deeply magical, richly fertile place wherein the dynamic interplay among creative imagination, playfulness and the therapeutic relationship can enable all manner of new possibilities to emerge. As I have said before, it is a place where anything can happen and where most things do. In relation to the use of self, it is a place where the play therapist has to exist in the moment, to take risks and be prepared for whatever direction this may take them; this is the child's journey after all, and who knows where it might lead? This intuitive sense of being in the moment, of working on the edge of one's awareness, requires a secure base from which to venture, and this comes only from training, experience and a developing sense of professional and personal self-awareness. To return to our earlier metaphor, if we are familiar enough with the main route then perhaps we can feel more confident about undertaking some exploratory forays down the lesser signposted pathways – knowing we can find our way back.

The psychotherapist Bugental (1987) describes this edge of awareness as a "dangerous place to be, an exciting place to work, a continually unsettling place to live subjectively" (1987: 95). To feel unsettled in this context is perhaps no bad thing, more a place of active imagination. The dynamic quality of a child's dramatic play means that as play therapists we are constantly on the edge of what we do and how we use our selves in the moment. This idea of working on the edge of awareness links also to the notion of therapeutic reverie, a process that evokes Bion's (1962) concept of maternal reverie and the idea that as therapists we sometimes find ourselves in that rather whimsical place of absent-minded (in the true sense of the word) musing or dreamlike contemplation about the meaning of the material, both client and therapist related, and the place where they meet in the middle.

The developing use of self: Questions of training, learning and experience

As said earlier, being a therapist is a developmental process, as is the therapeutic use of self. Understandably, in the early stages of our careers, as trainees or newly qualified therapists, there is a great deal more reticence and anxiety about the extent to which we actively bring ourselves into the work. Research by Skovholt and Rønnestad (1992) looked at the practice of therapists over a 10-year period and found that during their training and early post-qualifying years the therapists were much more reliant upon external support, for example adhering strictly to their particular theoretical orientation or drawing heavily upon their supervisor's style as a model or protocol for their own practice. Clearly, this is as it should be; one would hope and expect that the practice of trainees and newly qualified therapists of all disciplines is informed primarily by clinical supervision and their developing theoretical knowledge. In this sense, their practice is anchored by the twin pillars of knowledge and theory. But interestingly, the research also found that this strict adherence to theory was often at the cost of 'neutralising or suppressing' their own personality (Skovholt and Rønnestad, 1992). Further to this, some of the therapists involved in the study felt that their natural sense of humour was stifled or supressed during training, only resurfacing some time later after their training was completed for it to become integrated into their own developing practice.

In my experience, this is much the same with trainee and newly qualified play therapists wherein a strict adherence to a child-centred, non-directive theoretical orientation can create a degree of internal conflict as the trainee struggles to manage the tension between their professional and personal self. In the playroom, this can sometimes lead to an experience of feeling stuck or frozen, a little like the anxious rock climber who holds him or herself too close to the rock face; clinging on for safety but in the process unable to gain sufficient perspective to see the handholds and footholds from which to gain some further movement. Many times during the process of clinical supervision, I have heard a trainee play therapist say that their head was just too full of theory as they tried to find the right thing to do or say. I might suggest at these moments, somewhat counter-intuitively, that the trainee temporarily lets go of the theory and locate a sense of themselves; to try not to work so hard and allow space in the room for their own sense of self to emerge. I am reminded of Miles Davis, the seminal jazz trumpet player, who in the recording of the album *In a Silent Way* told John McLaughlin (one of the most technically accomplished jazz guitarists of his generation) to 'play like you don't know how to play'. McLaughlin subsequently produced a performance of sublime, intuitive simplicity. I also like the analogy of someone getting lost in the woods; instead of panicking and running faster and faster and becoming increasingly lost in the depths of the forest, it might be more helpful to simply stop, pause, take a look around and find one's bearings. Sometimes, to find one's way, it is about doing less not more.

So the play therapist's use of self is something that develops, grows and changes over time as we find flexible and creative ways to integrate theory and practice into our therapeutic *way of being*, to find compatible ways for the professional and personal to co-exist. As Skovholt and Rønnestad suggest in their study, the healthily developing therapist shows "an increasing closeness between the professional and personal selves in terms of being authentic at deeper levels of the self . . . the healthy evolution of the professional self permits the therapist to consistently meet one's own needs within an ethical, competent role" (Skovholt and Rønnestad, 1992: 105). So theory is not deserted or abandoned but instead integrated into a developing sense of professional identity that allows for one's own unique style and therapeutic presence to emerge. This takes us back once more to our metaphor of the road less travelled, that once we feel grounded enough in theory, experience and a sense of professional competence, we might allow ourselves to venture (or for the child to take us) 'off-piste' now and again, to see where the path may lead us.

Frameworks for the use of self

Clearly, it is important that the developing intuitive edge of professional practice is counterbalanced with relevant theory and that there is an ongoing reflexive flow between the two, one informing the other. Within the context of training, learning and professional development, there are a number of theoretical models that can help us consider the question of the therapeutic use of self.

In terms of self-awareness and personal insight, the Johari Window (Luft and Ingham, 1955) is a well-established psychological model for exploring self-awareness and the relationship between self and other. Within the framework of the Johari Window the *known self* is the area of the self that we can acknowledge and discuss with others, the open, shared view of ourselves. The *hidden self* (or façade) is that which we see or know about ourselves but others do not. It is a hidden area that might link to feelings of shame, vulnerability, strengths or simply things that about ourselves that we would rather not make known. The *blind self* is that part of ourselves that we do not see but that others do. It can be an area of incongruence, perhaps, wherein the perception we have of ourselves does not match with that of others. The unknown self is that part of ourselves that neither we nor others are consciously aware of. This may be in relation to unconscious, suppressed aspects of ourselves, both positive and negative. It is an area that could also perhaps be seen as connecting with the notion of the Jungian shadow, those parts of ourselves that we would least like to imagine.

Clearly, the greater our level of self-awareness and personal insight the greater our confidence in our practice as therapists and consequently our use of self. By definition, our blind spots are unknown areas but reflexive, self-aware practice means that throughout our work and with the support of clinical supervision and personal therapy, we are open to having a light shone upon these hidden, shadowy places so that they don't creep into our practice unbeknown. Returning to the experience of trainees, this is why self-awareness, insight and personal growth and development need to be a cornerstone of any play therapy training programme. As Rowan and Jacobs say, "much of the therapist's use of self consists of qualities, not skills . . . the way the therapist conducts themselves has its own impact upon clients: who the therapist is and the way the therapist relates may be as important as what the therapist says" (Rowan and Jacobs, 2002: 88).

Gardner and Yasenik's Play Therapy Dimension Model (2012) also provides a valuable framework for understanding the multi-dimensional nature of the play therapy process and the extent to which the therapist brings their *self* into the work. The model conceptualises the play therapy process according to two primary dimensions: directiveness and consciousness. Most of us would I think agree that these two fundamental dimensions lie at the heart of the play therapy process and encapsulate the perennial challenges that we experience as therapists in relation to how we seek to position ourselves along these two continuums and indeed why. In relation to the therapeutic use of self, Gardner and Yasenik's notion of *therapist immersion* is especially helpful, a quality they define as "the various ways and degrees to which the therapist engages in specific behaviours, language (verbal and non-verbal) and emotions during the play therapy session" (2012: 169).

A further model for looking at the use of self within play therapy, and in this instance congruence specifically, is the Experience-Expression Congruence Model (EECM) developed by Ray, Jayne and Stulmaker (2014). This model, recognising the complexity of congruence as a core therapeutic condition (or pre-condition), seeks to provide a conceptual framework to help play therapists understand the nature of congruence and to recognise its impact in therapy sessions whilst also aiming to intentionally use the play therapists awareness of congruence to benefit the child. Whilst the authors acknowledge the inherent difficulties in seeking to capture and express a complex construct like congruence in structural form, the EECM model does go some way towards helping the play therapist "navigate the balance of providing a therapeutic environment while also being an authentic person with the child" (2014: 29). The strength of this model is that it both acknowledges and allows openness to personal feelings as they emerge within the course of a session, facilitating the therapist in bringing their thoughts and feelings into conscious awareness wherein they can be thought about and evaluated in the context of the therapeutic relationship. It accepts that there will be moments or periods of incongruity and times when children perceive the therapist as inauthentic. This, as referred to earlier, is part of the relational ebb and flow of the therapeutic process, as it will invariably move back and forth on the congruence continuum.

The value of models such as these is that they provide us with supporting frameworks from which we can reflect upon the nature of our therapeutic presence within the playroom. They are also helpful within a supervisory context in the sense of informing our practice and providing a valuable counterbalance to our own clinical judgement. Although only touched upon briefly within this chapter, the role of clinical supervision is clearly fundamental to an ongoing understanding and awareness of how we apply ourselves to our therapeutic work. As well as being a place where links can be made between theory and practice, supervision also provides a place where the dilemmas, challenges, obstacles and opportunities in our therapeutic work with children can be explored and, most of all, where we can process our use of self within the playroom. After all, this work – as I have suggested – can lead us into unchartered territory.

Borders, boundaries and limits: Stretching the play therapy orthodoxy?

Several years ago now I worked as a therapist for looked-after children on the site of several local authority residential children's homes, a clustered community of nomadic young people who for many reasons were not able to be placed with foster carers. These were children with devastating histories of neglect, abuse and trauma, children who had experienced countless moves around the care system, been moved in and out of county and ultimately left with the invidious label 'unplaceable' hanging around their necks. These were also the children for whom the notion of being 'looked after' was something of a misnomer. Just to clarify, I don't mean this in the sense of the residential staff working in the residential homes, whose commitment, resilience and dedication to the lives of these children was second to none, but in the wider sense of the systemic, organisational dynamics that all too often saw children drifting between 'failed' placements with unclear care plans in ways that so often seemed to replicate their early family experiences.

Whilst these children's personal stories were driven by feelings of fear, anxiety, rejection and abandonment I was always struck by their energy, vitality, humour and resilience, and they taught me much about what it means to be a therapist, and in particular the importance of the relationship and, by definition, the therapeutic use of self. One recurring and pervasive aspect of this learning process was the dynamic relationship among containment, limit testing and therapeutic boundaries. These were young people who desperately sought emotional containment, the desire to be therapeutically held, but who would also understandably test any boundary they were confronted with, the frightened/frightening whose experiences of developmental trauma meant that ultimately, there was no safe place.

This often created unique challenges around how we managed to maintain the therapeutic relationship and with many children took me beyond the scope of what we might call the play therapy orthodoxy, by which I mean the acceptable, established, taught conventions of the play therapy process. Sometimes sessions were conducted outside the playroom, in the grounds of the children's homes, or we moved in and out of the playroom during the course of a session. I recall one young adolescent who would insist on bringing his bicycle into the session, which he would then ride in whirling circles around the playroom while I had to give him points for style and skill. One session took place sitting in a tree. In this sense, the relationship became the containing factor, not so much the room; and the flexibility in terms of how I used my self in these sessions, with the inherent risks involved, was key to the process of engaging with these young people. And within the playroom, my tolerance of mess (generally very high) was often taken to its limits as children sought ways to express the chaotic turmoil of their internal worlds and again far beyond what might be deemed acceptable.

The relationship between the therapeutic use of self and the maintenance of appropriate therapeutic boundaries is interesting; the idea that the need for congruency and authenticity in the relationship – to be real – can lead us to work in ways that we feel might not otherwise be permissible or conventional. Smith and Fitzpatrick state that "boundaries are regularly transgressed by even the most competent of therapists and such transgressions are not always to the detriment of the client" (1995: 500). They make a distinction between boundary crossing and boundary violation, the former being a term that describes 'departures from commonly accepted clinical practice that may or may not benefit the client' and the latter being a 'departure from accepted practice that places the client or the therapeutic process at serious risk'. So, in the immediacy of the work, one has to make finely balanced decisions about the active use of self in terms of how one might maintain or depart from the accepted norms of practice. Val Wosket talks about how she has become increasingly drawn to the 'rule breakers' who might work in unorthodox or intuitive ways that go beyond the confines of their training: "I have come to believe that rules can limit therapeutic effectiveness even as they also importantly define the boundaries of safe practice. Paradoxically, I have sometimes experienced the breaking of rules as seeming to provide an increase in safety and containment for clients" (1999: 133).

That said, I need to be clear that this is not about the absence of limits or boundaries but more a way of how they might be flexibly maintained in order to enhance the therapeutic process. Indeed, the experience of young people in the care system is that of boundaries being breached in all manner of ways – physically, emotionally and sexually – and in this sense limits and boundaries are a fundamental, critical and integral part of the play therapy process. But for many of the young people alluded to earlier, I am sure that had I stuck rigidly to play therapy conventions, they would never have engaged in any form of therapeutic process. As I have suggested earlier, with all aspects of the use of self, whether it relates to congruence, self-disclosure or boundaries and limits, the central issue is around having sufficient self-awareness and personal insight to know how these decisions are being informed and how they might impact the process. And of course the relationship is key – knowing the child well enough to make the kind of 'in-the-moment' decisions that can facilitate the therapeutic process in a way that is safe, containable and clinically sound.

So as said at the beginning of this chapter, the therapeutic use of self and intrinsic attitudinal core conditions of congruency and authenticity are complex, subjectively manifest and qualitatively difficult to evaluate. Who and how we are is as important as what we do, and in this sense the narrative thread of this chapter has more than anything been about play therapy as a *way of being* with children and within this an acknowledgment that we all bring our own, unique personal style into the work we do. Woven into this way of being are the influences of training, experience and theoretical orientation, all part of a dynamic process of learning as we continually integrate ongoing knowledge and experience into our developing practice. Ultimately, play therapy is about the relationship between therapist and child, and the more this can be experienced as an authentic, genuine and real relationship by the child the greater potential it has to be therapeutically healing.

References

Baldwin, M. (ed) (2000) *The Use of Self in Therapy*, 2nd Edn. New York: Haworth Press.

Barrett-Lennard, G. (1962) *Psychological Monographs: General and Applied*, 76, 1–36. Quoted in Ray, D., Jayne, K. & Stulmaker, H. (2014) A Way of Being in the Playroom: Experience-Expression Congruence Model (EECM). *International Journal of Play Therapy* Vol 23 (1), 18–30.

Bion, W. R. (1970) *Attention and Interpretation*. London: Tavistock.

Bion, W. R. (1962) *Learning from Experience*. London: Heinemann.

Bugental, J.F. (1987) *The Art of the Psychotherapist*. New York: Norton.

Gardner, K. & Yasenik, L. (2012) *Play Therapy Dimensions Model: A Decision-Making Guide for Integrative Play Therapists*. London: Jessica Kingsley.

Landreth, G. (1991) *Play Therapy: The Art of the Relationship*. Levittown, PA: AD Taylor Francis.

Lanyado, M. (2004) *The Presence of the Therapist: Treating Childhood Trauma*. Hove, New York: Brunner-Routledge.

Luft, J. & Ingham, H. (1955) The Johari Window: A Graphic Model of Interpersonal Awareness. *Proceedings of the Western Training Laboratory in Group Development*. UCLA.

Means, D. & Thorne, B. (2000) *Person Centred Therapy Today: New Frontiers in Theory and Practice*. London: Sage. Quoted in: Ray, D, Jayne, K. and Stulmaker, H. (2014) A

Way of Being in the Playroom: Experience-Expression Congruence Model (EECM). *International Journal of Play Therapy* Vol 23 (1), 18–30.

Ray, D., Jayne, K. & Stulmaker, H. (2014) A Way of Being in the Playroom: Experience-Expression Congruence Model *(EECM)*. *International Journal of Play Therapy* Vol 23 (1), 18–30.

Rogers, C.R. (1959) A Theory of Therapy, Personality and Interpersonal Relationships, as Developed in the Client-Centred Framework. In: Koch, S. (ed) *Psychology: A Study of Science*. Volume 3: 184–256. New York: McGraw-Hill.

Rowan, J. & Jacobs, M. (2002) *The Therapist's Use of Self*. Maidenhead: Open University Press.

Skovholt, T.M. & Rønnestad, M.D. (1992) *The Evolving Professional Self: Stages and Themes in Therapist and Counselor Development*. Chichester: Wiley.

Smith, D. & Fitzpatrick, M. (1995) Patient-Therapist Boundary Issues: An Integrative Review of Theory and Research. In: Wosket, V. (1999) *The Therapeutic Use of Self: Counselling Practice, Research, and Supervision*: 134. London: Routledge.

Van Fleet, R. Sywulak, A.E., Sniscak, C.C. & Guerney, L.F. (2010) *Child Centred Play Therapy*. London, New York: Guilford Press. Quoted in Ray, D., Jayne, K. & Stulmaker, H. (2014) A Way of Being in the Playroom: Experience-Expression Congruence Model (EECM). *International Journal of Play Therapy* Vol 23 (1), 18–30.

Wosket, V. (1999) *The Therapeutic Use of Self: Counselling Practice, Research, and Supervision*. London: Routledge.

Chapter 2

Can I really do this?

An exploration into therapist self-doubt

Elise Cuschieri

Preamble and introduction

The inception of this chapter, and the book that it forms a part of, occurred between discussions about lectures, marking dissertations and mugs of coffee, as David and I peered at each other over the tops of our computer screens at work. We discussed the need for a book that melded the theory and practice of play therapy with issues that, so far, had not featured much in the general literature in the field. That was fine. I enthusiastically threw ideas out and even ventured to suggest a subject area that I thought I could write about – one that I knew well, having experienced it so viscerally over many years . . . self-doubt, a critical inner voice, feeling incompetent.

All that was fine. I come from a family that does ideas very well. Many a Sunday lunch was spent discussing possibilities, potentialities and notions. When I was about seven years old, my father purchased a modest plot of land adjacent to our family home in Malta – "the field", as it came to be known – and for many years after that, this piece of land was the subject of much debate. Ideas were eagerly discussed: a swimming pool ("great for having friends round"), an orchard ("nice shade in the hot summer months"), a football pitch ("not large enough, balls might hit neighbours' windows"), a tennis court . . . suffice to say that some 40 years later, the field is still just that, a plot of land that gets over-grown in the winter months and parched and arid in summer, frequently becoming a fire hazard. So it was with some consternation that a few months after David and I batted book ideas around at work, I returned home to find a contract from Routledge popped through my letter box. My initial response was that something had gone seriously wrong. This was not how ideas are supposed to work. I had clearly underestimated my colleague's capacity for action.

So as I sit at my desk faced with the task of trying to write a chapter about a subject area that has been such a feature in my life prior to but most especially since training and qualifying as a play therapist, I realise that the attempt to articulate it immediately causes me to feel the very emotions I am hoping to explore and elucidate: inadequacy, insecurity, incompetence and a large dose of self-doubt. Feelings that I have endeavoured to keep in check, to 'conquer' and to rationalise over the years, so the thought of writing about them makes me feel vulnerable and exposed. Thus, while the main focus of this chapter will be an exploration of how these feelings may manifest themselves and are experienced when working as a play therapist, it would be disingenuous of me to ignore my own immediate responses to the process of *writing*; very similar emotions surge to the surface and cannot be denied or avoided. I hope that by acknowledging the feelings that emerge while writing and reflecting on the content, I can further my thinking and understanding and offer some perspectives on a subject that does not seem to be debated openly enough in the field of play therapy.

The first time I sat down at my desk, before even signing our book contract, I aborted the session after staring at a blank laptop screen for a whole morning; the only writing I could come up with at that stage was an expression of the angst I was already experiencing and knew, in all likelihood, I would continue to feel:

Ideas

Elusive

Slippery

Too many

Not enough

Blank screen

Nothing to say

Scared

Alone

Frozen

(2013)

I was aware, of course, that a great many writers describe feeling precisely this way about the process of writing. Even so, perhaps in my case this really was proof that I couldn't do it, that the process would be just too painful and agonising. I should say 'no' and back out as gracefully as I could. Strangely, though, and for reasons I still cannot fully articulate, I decided to go against my demanding and critical inner voice. I would not give in this time, I would persevere; rather than *fearing* the unhelpful feelings that I knew would surface, I resolved to consciously engage and start a dialogue with them. Instead of calling it a day whenever I became aware of self-doubt creeping in or my inner voice telling me I had nothing to say, I tried hard to be curious, to stay with the feelings rather than avoid them.

At the outset, I knew this process would have a heuristic quality to it, as I was aware that Douglass and Moustakas (1985: 40) define heuristic research as:

> . . . a search for the discovery of meaning and essence in significant human experience. It requires a subjective process of reflecting, exploring, sifting, and elucidating the nature of the phenomenon under investigation.

Moustakas (1990: 14) also states that "[i]n heuristic research the investigator must have had a direct, personal encounter with the phenomenon being investigated. There must have been actual autobiographical connections". These two elements of heuristic enquiry held particular resonance for me and have provided a way of framing my work for this chapter. I decided very consciously and deliberately to immerse myself in the thoughts, feelings and observations that arose as I started my exploration, bearing in mind the way Moustakas describes the process of immersion as an opportunity to "live it [question/area of focus] and grow in knowledge and understanding of it" (Moustakas, 1990: 28). I acknowledge, however, that while there is a heuristic quality to this enquiry, it is not a research study, which means that the phases of heuristic research as outlined by Moustakas (1990) serve as a broad framework rather than a tight methodology.

At the start of my enquiry into this area, I looked up the definition for self-doubt and found the following: "lack of confidence in oneself and one's abilities" (Soanes and Hawker, 2005: 935). While this provides a definition for 'self-doubt', I felt it failed to capture my experience as a play therapist. I recognise that I lacked confidence in the early stages of my training and as a novice therapist. However, as a more experienced therapist today, I feel a lack of confidence is not the full picture. Thus I decided to look up words connected to self-doubt to see if the synonyms threw any further light, but a search in the *Oxford Compact Thesaurus* (Waite, 2005: 443) revealed no entries for the word. I was surprised – maybe my process was over before it had even begun! I decided to extend my search and, instead, looked up 'insecurity' as I know there are moments when I may feel insecure in my role as a play therapist; I found the following list of synonyms:

SELF-DOUBT	DIFFIDENCE	UNASSERTIVENESS	TIMIDITY	UNCERTAINTY
NERVOUSNESS	INHIBITION	ANXIETY	WORRY	UNEASE

So there it was, self-doubt as a synonym for insecurity. I initially pondered on this and wondered what that meant for me as a play therapist, as a professional . . . Did I really want to reveal that part of me to others? These and many other thoughts were internally debated and jotted down in my journal. They did call into question what I was doing, but I also realised that I wanted to externalise something that I knew had caused me to struggle but had also served to push me to keep going. So I chose to continue.

These synonyms helped me begin to contextualise my experience of self-doubt as a play therapist and therefore give direction to this chapter: words such as 'diffidence', 'unassertiveness' and 'timidity' I knew straightaway were not part of my current experience, although I recognised them from my childhood and adolescent years. They were connected to my personal history of self-doubt but were not a part of my role as a play therapist. But the others struck more of a chord: uncertainty, along with feelings of anxiety, worry, unease and, sometimes, nervousness and inhibition; these seemed to elucidate emotional states that I recognise as having been present at times within my play therapy practice. For many years, I believed such feelings were my own personal demons to battle away at during personal therapy and clinical supervision. However, over the years, informally and anecdotally through discussions with colleagues and fellow play therapists, I have become aware that other therapists also experience self-doubt. This has gone some way towards helping me normalise these feelings and yet, despite this, I have continued to wonder about the impact that self-doubt and a critical inner voice can have on clinical practice. I am aware that at times, similar to my first abortive writing session for this chapter, these feelings are in danger of having a crippling or paralysing effect on me; they can seem to have the potential to stop me in my tracks, so that I feel there is no way forward. As a play therapist, I am aware of the negative impact on my work such responses could have if left unchecked, unacknowledged. So the decision to commit something to writing about the subject area is a personal risk, but it is borne out of a desire to shine a light on an area that seems important and yet, so far, largely ignored in play therapy literature.

A gradual process of engaging with the subject area has created an equally gradual start to this chapter. I wonder where this is going. The fact that the subject area touches me in a very personal way has led me to accept that it will have to develop somewhat organically. I am reminded of a butterfly struggling to emerge from a chrysalis and know the process will be similarly challenging. And yet, I have moved on from the angst of a blank screen in 2013; that is a huge step and gives me the impetus to carry on with the exploration. The mantra that was drummed into me and my fellow students while we were training seems especially apt: Trust the process.

In the following section of this chapter, I will present some research from adult psychotherapy that offers evidence of therapists' subjective experience of the feelings related to self-doubt. The decision to use research from adult psychotherapy rather than play therapy as a starting point is a necessary one: A review of play therapy literature appears to indicate that there has been no systematic enquiry to date with regard to how trainee, novice and/or experienced play therapists experience and manage self-doubt in their practice. In tandem with presenting research from adult psychotherapists' experiences, I will make some connections with child-centred play therapy (CCPT)[1] practice and theory. I will draw on my own experience as a play therapist but acknowledge the necessarily narrow and subjective perspective this offers. However, I hope it will serve to stimulate discussions about how feelings of self-doubt may emerge as a response to or result of therapeutic work with children and their families. I will also share some thoughts and ideas about what could help and what play therapists might do to avoid the *negative* effects of such feelings. In so doing, I hope to offer some initial perspectives on this phenomenon while acknowledging that a robust research project would be helpful in order to fully capture and elucidate play therapists' experiences of this area under discussion.

Definition

There have been numerous studies conducted in the related fields of clinical and counselling psychology and counselling and psychotherapy, which show that therapists experience self-doubt, question the effectiveness of their work and, as a result, can suffer stress and burnout throughout their careers (e.g., Farber and Heifetz, 1982; Deutsch, 1984; Mahoney, 1997; Orlinsky et al., 1999; Norcross, 2000; D'Souza et al., 2011). This area of research has largely focused on the influences and effects such factors have on aspects of the therapeutic process, for example, the therapeutic alliance and treatment outcomes. Other studies have made links between therapist self-doubt and the *quality* of the therapist–client alliance (e.g., Nissen-Lie et al., 2010; Nissen-Lie et al., 2013), while others still have demonstrated that the *person* of the therapist is a variable in treatment outcome, regardless of the therapist's theoretical orientation (e.g., Norcross and Wampold, 2011). Therefore, if the therapist *is* an accepted variable in the success or otherwise of treatment, it seems important to ask what happens to the *person* of the therapist when potentially damaging feelings arise from the work itself but also from the therapist's own life experiences, both historical and current.

As I investigated the subject, I knew I was interested in finding research that provided more of a *flavour* of the personal experience of self-doubt for therapists rather than quantitative studies. I was looking for research that somehow captured the visceral experience of self-doubt. I began to think that there were no such studies; perhaps therapists, generally speaking, have healthy and effective ways of coping with self-doubt, and if not, then the stress and possible burnout referred to above result in them leaving the profession. However, eventually I came across the phrase 'feelings of incompetence' as a collective term to refer to feelings related to self-doubt, inadequacy, insecurity and incompetence (Thériault, 2003). It would appear that Thériault was the first person to research the "subjective self-doubting process" (Thériault, 2003: 6) in a systematic manner, acknowledging that little attention had been given thus far to the therapist's personal experience of this phenomenon. Thériault and Gazzola (2005, 2006) have studied the *nature* and *sources* of feelings of incompetence in experienced therapists and, later on, in novice ones, too (Thériault, Gazzola and Richardson, 2009). In attempting to clarify these feelings, Thériault and colleagues (2009: 106) offer the following definition for feelings of incompetence (FOI):

> the emotions and thoughts that arise when therapists' beliefs in their abilities, judgements, and/or effectiveness in their role as therapists are reduced or challenged (. . .) FOI are the result of therapists' self-depreciating (*sic*), subjective evaluations of their own performances as practitioners; although they generally elicit anxiety, they can also be used for growth (i.e., FOI are not indicative of actual incompetent performance).

The above definition indicates that FOI can cause the therapist to feel uneasy or apprehensive about his[2] role and performance. Indeed, Thériault and colleagues (2009) draw attention to the levels of stress that can develop in new therapists due to FOI. They suggest that because FOI is not widely acknowledged or discussed, both in training programmes and in the literature, therapists can feel alone in their struggles and "erroneously equate FOI with incompetent performance, secretly thinking they are truly terrible therapists" (Thériault et al., 2009: 116). Thériault and colleagues (2009) also make the salient point that the general perception of therapeutic success tends to be "positively skewed" (Thériault et al., 2009: 116), with the emphasis in case studies, for instance, being on what worked, on successful outcomes and on 'best practice'. This can result in novice therapists concluding that their "insecurities are unusual and indicative of flawed practice" (Thériault et al., 2009: 116).

However, Thériault and Gazzola (2005) also make the point that FOI are not an indication of actual practice, that is, the therapist is not really incompetent but is experiencing *feelings* of incompetence as a result of engaging in a subjective negative judgement of his role and/or performance as a therapist. This seems an important point to note, and Thériault and Gazzola's research (2005, 2006) has clearly demonstrated that experienced therapists continue to experience self-doubt well into their careers. Thus FOI are not simply part of a normal developmental trajectory, such as might be expected in the case of therapists in training or those who have recently qualified. This raises the question of how such feelings are dealt with when, perhaps, they are perceived by the therapist or others to be unhelpful and possibly not acceptable.

However, it also appears there is a strong argument for FOI being regarded as an impetus for further professional growth and development, providing a way of keeping one on one's toes, as it were, for remaining alert and enquiring and for not becoming complacent or all knowing. Indeed, Thériault and Gazzola (2006: 326) note that "[t]he therapist's self-judgement can either fuel a healthy ambition to continuously evolve as a therapist or conversely be used as a weapon in a process of self-flagellation".

From data collated through semi-structured interviews with experienced therapists,[3] Thériault and Gazzola (2005) established a model with three main stages of FOI and two levels in each stage. The reported feelings ranged in "*depth* and *intensity*" [original emphasis] (2005: 13) from mild feelings of inadequacy [stage 1] through to feelings of insecurity [stage 2], and, finally, to what Thériault and Gazzola term "incompetence proper" [stage 3] (2005: 14), which aims to highlight the *experience* rather than provide a judgement of performance, as discussed. Thériault and Gazzola (2005) posit a series of questions for each level and use these to expand further on the three stages and their connected levels. What follows is a summary of each stage, with some links to child-centred play therapy practice for each of the three stages.

Stage 1: Being correct and effective (Thériault and Gazzola, 2005)

The first stage, in which feelings are mild and linked to inadequacy, the main preoccupation is with *being correct* [Level 1] and *being effective* [Level 2] (Thériault and Gazzola, 2005: 14). The focus is on the micro level, on the moment-by-moment exchanges between therapist and client with questions such as *Am I doing the right thing?* and *Am I able to help this client?* (Thériault and Gazzola, 2005: 14) being among the main preoccupations. Thériault and Gazzola (2005) suggest that such concerns are common but are mild in nature, leading therapists to feel inadequate at times during their practice but in a manner that does not affect their work and their own well-being.

Links to play therapy

In my quest to understand the above in the context of play therapy and to make sense of my own experience, I returned to the course journals I kept for the duration of my training as a play therapist. There I found evidence of self-doubt and FOI as I navigated the challenges of play therapy training, as the following journal extract indicates:

> *Whenever I am a therapist [in role play], I keep myself in check. I am afraid of putting a foot wrong, of making a mistake (. . .), so I stop myself from being 'me' (. . .). Perhaps it is not so much an issue of feeling unconfident but more perhaps a fear of being wrong, of making a mistake, and ultimately of harming a child.*
>
> *(Personal reflections for Play Therapy training course file, November, 2002)*

The concerns I allude to in the extract seem to suggest a feeling of inhibition, a sense of unease, echoing the synonyms I found at the start of this process. I recall, as a trainee and also a novice therapist, feeling inhibited at times, as a result of doubting my capacity to respond to the child in the most helpful way. I am reminded of the many questions that plagued my mind at the time: how should I 'track'[4]/what should I reflect/should I join in the child's play/how do I answer the child's questions/am I doing any of this right/am I getting it wrong/what will happen if I get it wrong/will I harm the child? At certain moments, my process of *becoming* a play therapist became hampered by doubt and ensuing anxiety: that I would inadvertently harm the child by a clumsy reflection or an ill-timed one; that I might hinder the therapeutic process if I joined in the play – or didn't join in . . . I recall that in the moment-to-moment interactions with a child, I sometimes found it hard to trust myself and my instinct, and the preoccupation with 'getting it right' would then take me away from the child to an internal space of self-questioning and self-doubt. I see this tendency of 'withholding' in my supervisory practice with trainee play therapists today; and I now realise that remaining silent out of fear of making a mistake can have, at times, more of a negative impact on the therapeutic relationship than the actual doing/saying something that the trainee may perceive to be mistaken, mistimed, misguided.

I know that as a trainee I believed and held onto the hope that once I had qualified and started practising, I would become less insecure about 'making mistakes' and ultimately more effective, that the feelings of incompetency and inadequacy would disappear. Today I recognise that although such feelings have not 'magically' disappeared, they have far less capacity to distract or to cause disengagement or detachment with the process. Nevertheless, there are still times when I question my practice, when I wonder whether I am being competent and effective. However, by becoming more aware of the impact of FOI and not feeling ashamed to discuss them, I am able to express and explore them more openly in the domains of clinical supervision and personal therapy as well as with trusted colleagues; and this has helped mitigate the potential negative effects.

Stage 2: Role and therapeutic process (Thériault and Gazzola, 2005)

The second stage includes issues around therapists' faith and confidence in their role [Level 3: *Am I a good therapist?* and *Somebody could do better than me*] (Thériault and Gazzola, 2005: 14) as well as questions about the therapeutic process and whether it actually works [Level 4]. FOI at this second stage move beyond the therapist wondering whether a particular exchange was helpful/effective or not to a deeper questioning of one's own capabilities as a therapist and the capacity or otherwise to trust the therapeutic process. Here the therapist may question whether he is the best person to help a particular client, whether he can be useful and effective while working with his client. When doubts about the actual process arise, about whether psychotherapy does in fact *help*, the therapist can start to feel insecure about his role as someone who 'helps'.

Links to play therapy practice

As a trainee on placement, I worked with a boy of six who was a selective mute. He chatted away at home but was silent in school and had been since starting nursery. His teacher wondered whether play therapy could help him, so I agreed to work with him but felt doubtful that I could have any effect with such a seemingly complex issue. I sat with this young child as he played silently, trying hard to follow his play and be with him. I was acutely aware of not putting pressure on him to 'talk' so was very careful about what I said, ensuring I avoided questions or any kind of 'I wonder . . .' comments in case he felt I wanted him to 'answer'. However, I frequently wondered to myself whether anything was 'happening', and this caused me to question whether I was on the right track and helping him. Towards the end of the 15 weeks, his teacher told me that he had started to talk to his friends in class. By the end of his sessions, he was talking to his teacher. I confess I was flabbergasted. Play therapy seemed to work!

As the above example illustrates, questions related to whether the process works have, especially in my early years of practice, been challenging for me and a source of FOI. At times, I have struggled with the CCPT process when I have had to manage the experience of 'not knowing', of not fully understanding what is going on in the play therapy session, perhaps because the child is playing out some aspect of her life experience that I do not, as yet, comprehend. In many ways, this is the very essence of child-centred play therapy: enabling the child to 'find her way' and trusting her process. However, I recognise that as a trainee or novice therapist, this can be challenging. I recall playing football with a child and wondering if it was 'play therapy', sitting with another child as she painstakingly filled every palette well with paint and wondering if I was really addressing her needs. In such moments, the desire to allocate meaning and to interpret, the pull to step in and 'direct' were strong. I may have known what I 'should' do, such as attuning, mirroring, facilitating expression through tracking and reflecting, empathising, but it was still a challenge. Maybe I could do more, hurry the process along, achieve quicker results if I introduced some form of direction or technique. I am aware that such situations have raised feelings of inadequacy and insecurity in me, and, at those times, remaining open and curious and 'staying with' rather than jumping ahead have been challenging. Once again, recognising them in supervision was an important part of my learning.

I am aware that questions about whether I am effective in my role as therapist and, more crucially, the right person for a particular child or family continue to exist for me today. In moments of doubt, I sometimes find myself wondering whether a specific child might fare better with my colleague, with a male therapist, with someone from the child's own ethnicity . . . I know I can come up with a long list of possible 'others', and yet I also know that experience has taught me to trust in my capacity to develop therapeutic relationships with children and to work effectively with families. However, by questioning whether my practice is competent and effective, I feel I continue to ensure that I do not become complacent or over-confident in my work. I believe these questions and others of a similar nature actually serve to 'keep me on my toes' rather than become a source of negative self-appraisal. Continuing professional development (CPD) activities, regular clinical supervision and experience have all helped me manage FOI in this area.

Stage 3: Contribution-attribution and a sense of identity (Thériault and Gazzola, 2005)

The third stage encapsulates "deeper levels of emotion as well as struggles with anxiety and anguish" (Thériault and Gazzola, 2005: 15). It would seem that whereas the preceding stage is related to the therapist's role, in the third stage the issues are related to "the core of the person, the self" (Thériault and Gazzola, 2005: 15). The main concern and focus at this stage is with what Thériault and Gazzola (2005: 15) term "contribution-attribution" [Level 5], where questions such as *Am I doing any good?*, *Am I doing any harm? Am I responsible for success?* and *Am I responsible for failure?* are asked. The issues arising here are challenging and involve the therapist assessing the impact of the work, the expectations that both client and therapist have, as well as how to gauge outcomes and success of treatment. Intense feelings can arise partly because the therapist may start to assume a great deal of responsibility for the work, perhaps more than is actually needed or indeed helpful for the client. In Level 6, the feelings are at their most intense, with Thériault and Gazzola (2005: 15) describing them as "[t]he most profound and disturbing level of self-doubt". Here the preoccupation is with the very person of the therapist and his "sense of identity and internal coherence" (Thériault and Gazzola, 2005: 15). Questions such as *Do I have what it takes?* and *What is wrong with me?* give some indication of the distress that such feelings can create (Thériault and Gazzola, 2005).

Links to play therapy practice

> *I feel very deskilled having listened to him (Garry Landreth) all day [. . .] it made me call into question all the children I have ever worked with and wonder if I've done any good or helped any of them at all. I feel frustrated that I seem to [. . .] feel inadequate and incompetent so quickly. I feel such a fraud . . .*
>
> *(Personal journal, November 2013)*

The above extract was written following a training day with Garry Landreth at the University of Roehampton. I recall enjoying and being stimulated by the day, and yet when I went home, I reflected on my play therapy practice and started to query what I had done over the years, whether I had what it takes and whether I had any right being a play therapist. Such questions and doubts, when they arise in me, seem to go to my very core, and I am aware that the third stage described above has a particular resonance for me in my work with vulnerable children. I know I have a tendency to question myself, to be self-critical and to always want to do a better job. These are personal traits that were around long before I became a play therapist and are intricately linked to my personal history. However, I am also aware that, since I became a play therapist, such traits seem to have manifested themselves more acutely in my work.

I have wondered a lot about the above: What is it about play therapy that creates such a different response in me to other work I have done in the past with children, some of whom were also vulnerable? During the course of this exploration, I came across the following perspective by Bonovitz, a child psychotherapist (2009: 239), who acknowledges that child therapists are especially disposed to "[t]he sense of parental responsibility, protectiveness, and concerns with doing harm or damage" when working with vulnerable child clients, as compared to therapists working with adults. This immediately had resonance for me and I recognise the potential in me and in others to be 'drawn in' which is, I believe, intricately linked to personal characteristics, vulnerabilities and life history.

I know that at times I am drawn into taking on too much responsibility for a child's emotional or psychological well-being. For instance, the multiple systems in which many children are embedded, such as family, school, social care or other professional agencies, all give rise to particular complexities within the work. Although I know engagement with the child's family and liaising with other professionals connected to the child are vital aspects of the work, these activities have the capacity, at times, to raise anxieties in me as I grapple with questions such as who is responsible for what, who/what can make a difference for the child and how do I preserve the therapeutic relationship with the child without being pulled out of role or taking on too much responsibility. I am aware that such dilemmas can prove to be a source of FOI, and here, both clinical supervision and personal therapy offer ways of moderating the negative effects.

The three stages: A brief summary

The three stages and allied levels described offer a framework for thinking about the breadth and depth of feelings connected to self-doubt. Two key factors that emerge from the research seem important to note: (1) according to the level of intensity, FOI can cause concomitant feelings of anxiety and distress in therapists; and (2) the findings indicate that such feelings are an ongoing and integral part of being a therapist, regardless of length of experience. Thus, to sum up, FOI can have a detrimental effect on the *person* of the therapist, not only on one's 'performance'; and the feelings do not necessarily go away with time or experience (Thériault and Gazzola, 2005).

Self-doubt and CCPT theory

Having reflected on each of Thériault and Gazzola's three stages and made links to my practice, I wondered what some of the key proponents of CCPT say about the personal challenges that play therapists may face. As discussed earlier, there do not appear to be any research studies focusing on self-doubt in play therapists. Thus I have drawn on some core texts from CCPT.

Cochran, Nordling and Cochran (2010), in their comprehensive guide to developing therapeutic relationships with children in play therapy, make reference to the personal challenges that play therapists may face in their work. For instance, in seeking to address the novice play therapist's professional development, Cochran and associates warn their reader that there will be times of "personal struggle – where you begin to lose heart" (2010: 383). They suggest this will surface as a response to the difficult and sad situations that many child clients have experienced. This seems to hint at the risks of therapist burnout as a result of the emotional impact the work can have and the toll this can take.

Cochran and colleagues (2010) also discuss what happens when, as a response to the child's difficult life experiences, the child-centred play therapist tries *too* hard to alleviate the suffering of the child he is working with. They suggest that the therapist may unwittingly run the risk of prolonging the very suffering he is seeking to end. Cochran and colleagues (2010) postulate that this can happen when the play therapist starts to take responsibility for growth and healing away from the child, which can curtail the child's opportunities for mastery as well as for seeking out and discovering her own internal resources. Instead of the child finding her own way forward with the therapist facilitating this process, the therapist takes over responsibility, becoming perhaps more directive than facilitative. This seems to echo the notion of 'contribution-attribution' as defined by Thériault and Gazzola (2005: 15) in which, in an effort to manage the impact that a therapeutic process may have on the therapist, he becomes more reliant on techniques and less trusting of the process.

Ray (2011: 71), on the other hand, reflects on one of the core elements of CCPT, congruence,[5] and states that it is "intimately correlated with the therapist's self-awareness and sense of self. A lack of self-regard leads some play therapists to cover up feelings of inadequacy, replacing these feelings with a façade of competence". Ray acknowledges her own struggles with self-regard, which she attributes to conditions of worth, and recognises that a lack of self-acceptance can impact on her capacity to provide genuine acceptance and unconditional positive regard to the child clients she works with (Ray, 2011). This acknowledges clearly that personal vulnerabilities and one's own history can be sources of FOI.

Landreth (2002) provides a comprehensive picture of the qualities and characteristics needed to be a play therapist. He cites, amongst others, the importance of being "*personally secure*" [original emphasis] (Landreth, 2002: 101), having an awareness of and ability to understand one's own actions and, as Ray also emphasises, to be accepting of oneself. Landreth reiterates the need for all therapists to be engaged in active self-exploration and to have "insight into their own motivations, needs, blind spots, biases, personal conflicts, and areas of emotional difficulty as well as personal strengths" (Landreth, 2002: 102). He highlights the importance of child-centred therapists utilising personal and/or group therapy as a means of enhancing self-understanding and of accessing clinical supervision to support their play therapy practice. Landreth does not directly discuss the issue of self-doubt or how one might respond to feelings of incompetence that may arise while working with vulnerable children; but this is, perhaps, because he views the active engagement in self-exploration to be the counterpoint to mitigating the negative effects of such feelings. This seems a vital aspect to bear in mind and seems to link to what has been discussed.

Of all the play therapy literature that I returned to in my preparation for this chapter, Landreth's depiction of a child-centred play therapist was the one that made me stop short and question my reasons for writing this chapter. Why am I grappling with self-doubt, then, so many years after first being inspired by Landreth's dynamic description? Shouldn't I be beyond this? After so many years of regular supervision and engagement with personal therapy, shouldn't I, by now, fit Landreth's description and be able to deal effectively with any feelings of self-doubt? I love being a child-centred play therapist; I believe in the innate capacity of children to express difficult life experiences through their play; and I have faith in the power of play to heal and in the therapeutic relationship that is developed anew with every child. And yet I am also aware that, sometimes, in my work as a child-centred play therapist, I can feel very self-critical as I strive to be the very best for each child I encounter.

Almost immediately the awareness of all this threatens to have a paralysing effect on me and my writing. What can I possibly have to say when I have clearly not lived up to Landreth's exhortations? Perhaps this is the end of the road. It has a pleasing cyclical nature to it, if nothing else . . . Landreth's "The Art of the Relationship" was the first play therapy text through which I felt 'this is it, this is what I want to do, this is what I want to become'. Perhaps this is where I bow out . . . Stacking shelves has a comforting appeal.

This experience really did stop me in my tracks. I stopped writing for a few days, feeling weary, despondent and beaten. The process of discovery had finally collided with the process of engagement. I felt I couldn't carry on. The book would have to have one chapter less.

But the chapter is here, so I clearly ploughed on . . . and it certainly felt like ploughing. I was tired, and I was still very doubtful that I should be doing this. It took a conversation with someone who is not a therapist to help me reframe my response to Landreth's writing, to help me to see that what Landreth was describing was, perhaps, an ideal, a model, a composite depiction of the best. In my response to Landreth's model, I was disregarding human fallibility as well as the notion of process; that one does not just 'become' a play therapist but rather continues to evolve over time; it is not an all or nothing approach. I may have been practising for more than a decade but I am still very much engaged in the creative process of 'becoming', with each new relationship that develops with a child, each new family, each personal experience all impacting on and melding with my whole being. So rather than viewing this process of exploration and writing as a success or failure – a rigid set of polarities that I have been inclined to apply in the past – I could persevere and continue to allow the process to unfold without being such a harsh self-critic. I could, perhaps, also entertain the notion of the 'good-enough therapist' rather than striving to be the mythical 'perfect therapist'.

A synthesis of the process

The following section is an attempt to draw together the research on FOI and how that research can inform ways of thinking about self-doubt and FOI for play therapists. In trying to utilise the research to help me understand my own experience, I found it useful to think about my feelings along a continuum. I have reflected on how self-doubt manifests itself in different ways and how it varies in intensity. This has led me to create the following paradigm (see Figure 2.1) as a way of understanding the different types of feelings associated with self-doubt and FOI and the manner in which they can change according to their intensity. I have constructed the paradigm with the four zones, along with the descriptive words that illustrate the different zones. I see it as a kind of synthesis of my process in writing this chapter, echoing the "creative synthesis" that Moustakas (1990: 31) describes.

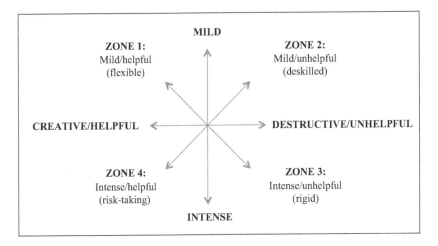

Figure 2.1 The Self-Doubt Paradigm

The Self-Doubt Paradigm: Some observations

The above model has given me a framework for thinking about what happens when self-deprecating feelings become activated. I have found it has helped me to further understand the different feelings and how these may shift and transform, both along the horizontal axis, in terms of the *nature* of the feelings, but also along the vertical axis, where movement is brought about according to the *strength* of the feelings. It seems to me that movement can take place in all directions: left to right along the horizontal axis as well as right to left; up and down on the vertical axis but also down-up, when the feelings shift back to a milder form from having been experienced more intensely; diagonal movement seems also possible when feelings might shift in nature and intensity from, for instance, Zone 3 to Zone 1.

In the following section, I attempt to make some generic links to practice. I will then offer two examples from practice in order to further understand the ways in which these feelings may manifest themselves in play therapy practice. Once again, due to the absence of research in this area, the following are based on my own observations and experiences from my play therapy practice. I hope that they can serve to stimulate thought and discussion rather than provide any kind of definitive statement.

As a general observation, I would say that I sometimes experience FOI as being helpful (Zone 1). I might feel challenged by a session I have just had with a child or an encounter with a parent/carer. I may feel unsure about whether I was helpful in an interaction with a professional or experience uncertainty about my capacity to work with the challenges expressed. However, in these situations, I am open to the work and feel stimulated and energised. As I have come to conceive it, this type of self-doubt/FOI serves to keep me 'on my toes', to remain connected, engaged and dynamic.

At other times, the feelings seem less helpful, such as occasions when I find it more of a challenge to remain open to the ambiguity or complexity of the work; when I feel pulled into thinking that I *could* be doing more, *should* be working harder, ought to be doing things differently; when I feel deskilled and pulled away from trusting the child and the process. In these situations, the feelings are still relatively mild insofar as they tend to be kept out of the therapeutic space and reflected on in personal notes or supervision. But they certainly have a less helpful quality to them; I now conceptualise these as a move along the horizontal axis towards Zone 2.

I am aware that, on occasion, the feelings that arise in me tap into the core of my being (Zone 3). The feelings may be in response to complex cases, such as a young person who is self-harming or a child who has experienced trauma, but they may also be linked to personal issues or circumstances at a given time. On these occasions, it seems that my personal life can create feelings of vulnerability within me, and these have the potential to 'collide' with my professional life. Similar to Thériault and Gazzola's description of 'Stage 3', it is then that I doubt myself profoundly, my capacity to do the work and, most fundamentally, my suitability. At those moments, I may feel less open and more rigid in my work, causing me to question whether I am skilled or competent enough to engage in the deep and moving work that is required of me. I now perceive my task at these times to be one of transforming those pernicious, unhelpful feelings into something that is no less intense but can be worked with and can challenge me to continue, to be creative in my work, to trust in myself, in the process and in the child. I consider this as a move from Zone 3 to Zone 4. This has been a helpful realisation, and it has assisted me in recognising that although my critical inner voice has not entirely disappeared, over the years engagement in regular clinical supervision and in personal therapy have supported me in finding ways to utilise it in a manner that can be creative and helpful (Zone 4).

The following two case examples[6] from my practice in recent years might help to illustrate some of the above points and the possible movement amongst the four zones. I have tracked the movement retrospectively after creating 'The Self-Doubt Paradigm' on page 31.

Billie was nine years old when he was referred for play therapy. He lived with his father, two older brothers and one younger sister; his mother had had a history of alcohol dependence and depression and died from an apparent overdose of prescription drugs a year and a half before I met Billie. He was referred for play therapy due to challenging behaviour at school, getting into fights with peers, refusing to comply with school rules and routines and a long list of other 'misdemeanours'. His father reported a different picture. Billie was, if anything, quiet at home, his father's "little trouper".[7] Billie had night-time enuresis and did not want to sleep alone at night.

Quite quickly into our sessions, Billie found a sponge ball in the playroom. His eyes lit up, and he asked if we could play football together. Up until finding the ball, Billie had struggled to engage in any sustained play activity. I had reflected on Billie's uncertainty about being in the room and about the difficulty in deciding what to do while Billie had lamented the lack of anything technological in the playroom. *Perhaps football would offer a 'way in'. Or perhaps it would prove to be an avoidance strategy, a way of keeping me at bay; perhaps it would take us away from play where Billie might be able to express difficult emotions.* All this and more whizzed around my head as Billie and I contemplated the sponge ball he had just found (*Zone 1*).

The next six to eight sessions were intense and energetic as Billie and I found ways to negotiate our growing relationship together. Quite quickly a pattern emerged in our sessions: I was shouted at for not kicking the ball 'right', for not tackling 'right', for being offside, for not doing a good job as goalie; I was booked, sent off . . . the list was endless, and fairly rapidly I started to feel inadequate and not good enough. I could not get it right for Billie; he was getting more and more frustrated with me. In a moment of stereotypical thinking, I recall contemplating that Billie would be better off with a male play therapist. They were challenging times and frequently made me question whether I was responding in the best way to Billie's needs, whether this would have any meaningful impact on him, for him, on our relationship, on our process, whether football 'worked' in play therapy (*Zone 2, with possible shift to Zone 3*).

However, almost as rapidly as the feelings of inadequacy and incompetence rose up in me, I became aware that these feelings were a response to the dynamic relationship developing between Billie and me, that the feelings were much more about Billie's experience than my competence or otherwise as a play therapist – or footballer. This awareness helped me to take some risks (*Zone 2 to Zone 4*), as I responded to Billie in a way that opened up a dialogue between us. In amongst the energetic kicks, side tackles and missed goals, I started to reflect gently on what was happening between us, beginning with my own experience of 'getting it wrong' in football and reflecting on how hard it is to be always 'wrong'. It felt risky; I was being explicit about my experience, about what was emerging between us in the moment, and I was inviting Billie to wonder about his own experience. However, Billie responded to this, and through our football games, he was able to explore some of his difficult experiences and feelings in a non-threatening manner. Our work together continued for several months, and in that time Billie found other creative ways to express himself, especially through role play. However, we returned to football many more times, and it was certainly a means for Billie to explore his many thoughts and feelings about his experiences, including his mother's death.

Rosie was seven years old at the time of referral, and she lived alone with her mother. Rosie had intermittent contact with her father, who misused drugs. There was a history of domestic abuse between Rosie's parents and issues about her father having contact with Rosie. Rosie was referred to play therapy due to separation anxiety and general anxiety. She was 'clingy' with her mother, hated going to school and frequently said she had tummy aches, headaches, and other possible psychosomatic symptoms; Rosie had night-time enuresis and found it difficult to fall asleep at night, worried that someone might be lying under her bed or would come through the window to 'get her'.

Rosie's early play therapy sessions were characterised by intense colouring in of pictures, a lack of eye contact with me, almost complete silence on her part and sudden departures from the room – to show her mother something in the waiting area, to go to the toilet, to give her mother something, to wash her hands. There was never any warning that Rosie was going out of the room; she would just go. I was puzzled by her behaviour, as I had never worked with a child who found it so hard to remain in the room for an entire session, but I was convinced we would find a way forward together (*Zone 1*). During her third session, and after many clumsy attempts at reflecting on her need to leave the room, including 'you want to check the outside is still there', I reflected on her *mother*'s need to see Rosie was still there; previously I had only focused on Rosie's needs. Rosie's response to this comment was to make fleeing eye contact, and a hint of a smile? This seemed to provide a 'way in'. It made me realise that Rosie was acutely aware of her mother's anxiety as well as trying to manage her own fears and worries.

The next session, Rosie went straight to a box containing collage materials. She found string and masking tape and used these to join together, stick and bind anything she could find and use in the playroom. She tied toys and pieces of furniture together, creating elaborate web-like patterns across the length and width of the playroom. She moved around the room with urgency and purpose. This was a very different little girl to the initial sessions. I was intrigued by the process but wondered whether I was going to be helpful to her (*Zone 1*). Gradually Rosie started to involve me in her play, ordering me to "stick that bit there, Elise" and "make a knot here, Elise".

Increasingly, over a number of weeks, the orders became peremptory commands with Rosie shrieking, "come here, Elise, no NOT there, HERE", "do this, no not like that, LIKE THIS", "can't you do anything right?" It seemed that no matter how hard I tried, my efforts were never satisfactory, never enough. I was berated and chastised and began to feel helpless and hopeless. *I questioned whether I was being effective in my work with Rosie. Was I helping her? Was I competent enough? Was anything going to shift for Rosie, or was the process not working? Maybe Rosie needed a different therapist (Zone 2 shifting to Zone 3).* When I reflected on her sessions and discussed them in supervision, I knew my feelings were stemming from Rosie's experiences, but it was sometimes hard work to remain open and relaxed in the sessions. I often felt deskilled and at times was aware of feeling anxious and rigid, but regular supervision helped me remain focused on Rosie's process. It also helped me manage my feelings of vulnerability and doubt (*Zone 3 to Zone 4*) and remain flexible and engaged with Rosie.

Gradually, the frenzied tying and sticking together of objects evolved into role play that extended over a number of weeks, where Rosie was the princess and I was the lady-in-waiting. We were tied up, trapped and in need of being rescued, or we were barricaded in (door frame and handle firmly taped up by Rosie – no more hasty flights), protecting ourselves from the marauding soldiers outside, princess and lady-in-waiting safe against the world.

The work with Rosie continued for several months after the play described briefly. It contained many twists and turns, including social care and police. The above case raised many feelings of doubt and anxiety in me and, on reflection I can see that I moved amongst all four zones during the course of the work. But I also realise that most of the more intense feelings arose not out of the direct work with Rosie but because of the many professional systems that became involved in the case and their attempts to pull me out of my role and to threaten the relationship Rosie and I had firmly built together. For the most part, the play therapy room remained a protected space for Rosie where she found wonderfully creative means to play out the complex and often perplexing issues in her life.

I didn't always get it right for Rosie; there were times when she would again shout "not like that, Elise" or would respond with a dismissive "no I don't" if I tried to reflect on a feeling and my timing was out of sync or simply off the mark. But our relationship grew steadily and, with that, developed an increasing capacity on both our parts to be open about the process we were engaged in. I could revisit 'misses' and 'mismatches' with Rosie and she, I believe, experienced me as an adult who didn't always 'get it right' with her, but we could talk about that without guilt, fear or shame. I think that was important for Rosie, given the complexities of her experiences with the other adults in her life. It was certainly one of those cases that on paper seemed relatively straightforward but that, once the work deepened, proved to be a complicated web of relationships and experiences that was challenging for a young child to untangle. Rosie immersed herself wholeheartedly in an intense and creative process. I felt and still feel humbled to have been a part of it.

Concluding thoughts

Writing 'Concluding thoughts' has a strange feel; I cannot quite believe that I have got here. An idea has come to fruition . . .

I hope this chapter has served to shine a light on an area that, to date, has had little direct treatment in play therapy literature. I recognise that it is a subject that is somewhat inviolable, that has a trace of the taboo about it, and yet by leaving it off-limits, as it were, I think there is a risk of play therapists unnecessarily carrying the weight of intense feelings and of practice being negatively impacted. My own experience of finding ways to be honest with peers, colleagues and, critically, myself about such feelings has proved vital for me; it seems to be a crucial way of seeing FOI in the right context: by allowing others to contribute to a process of vital self-reflection and evaluation. Thus it would seem that one way for the individual, whether trainee, novice or experienced therapist, to really understand and manage self-doubt and FOI is by engaging in open and candid discussions with, for instance, clinical supervisors, personal therapists and/or other trusted play therapists. I have also come to believe that this subject needs to be included in play therapy training programmes so that trainees are helped to find strategies to manage such feelings at the start of their practice. There are, of course, other ways to mitigate the potential negative effects: Self-care is a critical element in the way in which play therapists can manage feelings related to self-doubt; and the manner in which play therapy sessions and the emotional impact of them are processed also seems important to consider. However, these areas of discussion are, perhaps, for another time.

I have come to believe that continuing to experience FOI can be positive, that self-doubt and feelings of incompetence can be a reminder and an indication of my humanity. The role of compassion in the work with vulnerable children and young people cannot be overstated, and I believe that in a strange way, self-doubt can serve to ensure that care and concern remain at the heart of what I do and why I chose this profession. I strongly believe that consideration for the well-being of others and one's own humane responses to others need never be at odds with the quest for greater professionalism, for managing boundaries, for coping with the emotional demands of the work. In the end, it seems to me that self-doubt and FOI *can* be helpful, can be the impetus for further learning and development and can engender a more flexible and creative response to the work. However, I have also come to believe, even more strongly than ever before, that for this to even start to happen, one needs to "[t]o know oneself in truth and fully" Moustakas (1997: 17).

Notes

1 As a child-centred play therapist, the theoretical perspective that I draw on is based on child-centred play therapy theory; however, I hope that therapists with different theoretical viewpoints may also find this chapter helpful.
2 For the sake of clarity I will use the male pronoun to denote the therapist and the female pronoun to denote the client (adult or child).
3 Inclusion in the study required participants to have more than 10 years' experience in psychotherapeutic practice (Thériault, 2003).
4 Tracking is a key skill in CCPT; for more information, see Landreth (2002).
5 The other two are empathy and unconditional positive regard, as outlined by Rogers and upon whose theory Virginia Axline (1989) first developed non-directive play therapy.
6 All cases are anonymised and drawn from composite material in order to maintain confidentiality.
7 All quotes are taken from personal case notes.

References

Axline, V. M. (1989) *Play Therapy*. London: Churchill Livingstone.

Bonovitz, C. (2009) Countertransference in Child Psychoanalytic Psychotherapy: The Emergence of the Analyst's Childhood. *Psychoanalytic Psychology* Vol 26 (3), 235–245.

Cochran, N. H., Nordling, W. J. & Cochran, J. L. (2010) *Child-Centered Play Therapy: A Practical Guide to Developing Therapeutic Relationships With Children*. Chichester: John Wiley.

Deutsch, C. J. (1984) Self-Reported Sources of Stress Among Psychotherapists. *Professional Psychology: Research and Practice* Vol 15 (6), 833–845. http://dx.doi.org/10.1037/0735–7028.15.6.833 (accessed 29/12/14).

Douglass, B. & Moustakas, C. (1985) Heuristic Inquiry: The Internal Search to Know. *Journal of Humanistic Psychology* Vol 25 (3), 39–55.

D'Souza, F., Egan S. J. & Rees C. S. (2011) The Relationship Between Perfectionism, Stress and Burnout in Clinical Psychologists. *Behaviour Change* Vol 28 (1), 17–28. http://dx.doi.org/10.1375/bech.28.1.17 (accessed 29/12/14).

Farber, B. A. & Heifetz, L. J. (1982) The Process and Dimensions of Burnout in Psychotherapists. *Professional Psychology* Vol 13 (2), 293–301. Available at: http://psycnet. apa.org (accessed 03/09/14).

Landreth, G. L. (2002) *The Art of the Relationship*. New York: Brunner-Routledge.

Mahoney, M. J. (1997) Psychotherapists' Personal Problems and Self-Care Patterns. *Professional Psychology: Research and Practice* Vol. 28 (1), 14–16. Available at: http:// psycnet.apa.org (accessed 29/12/14).

Moustakas, C. (1997) *Relationship Play Therapy*. Lanham, MD: Rowman & Littlefield.

Moustakas, C. (1990) *Heuristic Research: Design, Methodology and Applications*. London: Sage.

Nissen-Lie, H. A., Monsen, J. T. & Rønnestad, M. H. (2010) Therapist Predictors of Early Patient-Rated Working Alliance: A Multilevel Approach. *Psychology Research* Vol 20 (6), 627–646.

Nissen-Lie, H. A., Monsen, J. T., Ulleberga P. & Rønnestad, M. H. (2013) Psychotherapists' Self-Reports of Their Interpersonal Functioning and Difficulties in Practice as Predictors of Patient Outcome. *Psychotherapy Research* Vol 23 (1), 86–104. http://dx.doi. org/10.1080/10503307.2012.735775 (accessed 03/09/14).

Norcross, J. & Wampold, B. E. (2011) Evidence-Based Therapy Relationships: Research Conclusions and Clinical Practices. *Psychotherapy* Vol 48 (1), 98–102 (accessed 03/09/14).

Norcross, J. C. (2000) Psychotherapist Self-Care: Practitioner-Tested, Research-Informed Strategies. *Professional Psychology: Research and Practice* Vol 31(6), 710–713. http:// dx.doi.org/10.1037/0735–7028.31.6.710 (accessed 03/09/14).

Orlinsky, D., Rønnestad, M. H., Ambühl, H., Willutzki, U., Botersman, J.-F., Cierpka, M., Davis J. & Davis, M. (1999) Psychotherapists' Assessments of Their Development at Different Career Levels. *Psychotherapy: Theory, Research, Practice, Training* Vol 36 (3), 203–215. http://dx.doi.org/10.1037/h0087772 (accessed 29/12/14).

Ray, D. C. (2011) *Advanced Play Therapy*. New York: Brunner-Routledge.

Soanes, C. & Hawker, S. (eds.) (2005) *Compact Oxford English Dictionary*, 3rd Edn. Oxford: Oxford University Press.

Thériault, A. (2003) *Therapists' Feelings of Incompetence: A Grounded Theory Analysis of Experienced Clinicians* (Unpublished PhD manuscript).

Thériault, A. & Gazzola, N. (2005) Feelings of Inadequacy, Insecurity, and Incompetence Among Experienced Therapists. *Counselling and Psychotherapy Research* Vol 5 (1), 11–18.

Thériault, A. & Gazzola, N. (2006) What Are the Sources of Feelings of Incompetence in Experienced Therapists? *Counselling Psychology Quarterly* Vol 19 (4), 313–330.

Thériault, A., Gazzola, N. & Richardson, B. (2009) Feelings of Incompetence in Novice Therapists: Consequences, Coping and Correctives. *Canadian Journal of Counselling* Vol 43 (2), 105–119.

Waite, M. (ed.) (2005) *Oxford Compact Thesaurus*, 3rd Edn. Oxford: Oxford University Press.

Chapter 3

Reflections on gender

The male play therapist

David Le Vay

> Most men lead lives of quiet desperation and go to the grave with the song still
> in them.
>
> – H. D. Thoreau

I recall, many years ago now, arriving for the first day of my play therapy training and realising that I was the only male in residence, an experience that I am
sure many male play therapists will be able to recognise. Ann Cattanach, the
programme convenor, gave me a somewhat knowing look and gently inquired
as to my well-being, the sub-text clearly being about my ability to manage my
minority of gender status. 'I'll be fine', I told her, and so I was. But it was an
odd, unique experience, often challenging and sometimes isolating, but overall a
deeply rewarding and insightful period in my life.

I also recall when working with a team that provided therapeutic support for
children with sexually harmful behaviour, again as the sole male, the new manager inquired during supervision about what it felt like to be the only man in the
team. 'It must make you want to chop your penis off', she said. *Not especially*, I
thought, *but it sounds like you might want to*. Did I have to emasculate myself to
work here or be emasculated by others? Was this about gender, power, sex? Did I
have to be symbolically castrated – neutered – to enforce my own sexual neutrality and render me safe? And of course the context of my work with adolescent
sexual offenders was pertinent, an arena wherein (male) sexuality is dangerous
and abusive, a form of attack. 'Lay down your weapons' was perhaps the sub-
text, if you want to become 'one of us'. And indeed, what is my own story about
stumbling into a career within which I am working primarily alongside women
and with children primarily abused by men? What is my own narrative identity
around masculinity and the meaning of 'maleness'?

My aim within this chapter is to explore these questions: the territory of gender
within play therapy and, specifically, what it means to be a male play therapist
within a profession that has come to be socially constructed as predominately

female. What does this say about the role of men in society and indeed of society's view of men who seek to work professionally with children? The currency of child abuse is now a precious media commodity, feeding a growing anxiety around children's welfare and a culture of suspicion and unease as the grainy, re-visited faces of 'celebrity paedophiles' stare out at us, dead eyed, from the front pages of our newspapers. And what does it mean to be a male therapist working with children who have experienced abuse and trauma within a family context where men are mostly absent or abusive? And perhaps most of all, what are the stories that get played out in the therapeutic play space and within the relationship, and how are these stories informed by gender?

To put this discussion into some kind of context we need to look at the socio-economic, cultural and perhaps even political lens through which childhood (and childcare) is viewed within the UK. Of course this is complex; gender roles are powerfully defined, stereotyped and reinforced in many ways and the notion of sexual equality, something that we would all clearly aspire to, still remains somewhat elusive as long as the economic and political institutions of the day continue to remain primarily within the male domain. Society, I would suggest, is far from equal, and so gender identity, who, how and what we are, is also powerfully shaped by the explicit and implicit forces that inform our daily lives. And these forces also contribute to the ongoing social construction of childhood and how and by whom our children are cared for and also, I would suggest, to the emergence of play therapy as a profession, itself in its early, developing years.

What are the societal perceptions of men who play with children? A report by the London Early Years Foundation (2012) on men working in childcare talks about the absence of men in the fields of teaching and childcare being a consequence of 'multiple factors related to the perceived feminised nature of early years work' (Sargent, 2005). Further research (Cameron, 2001; Cameron and Moss, 2004) highlights a number of themes that underpin the limited presence of men within the field of early years, perhaps the most significant being that to do with the overall perception of men within society and the prevailing social narrative that working with children is a predominantly female profession, a perception or construction that reinforces and perpetuates gender patterns of employment, training and recruitment.

As said, the factors involved in this area are multiple and complex. Research (Blount, 2005) also suggests that whilst women are viewed as nurturers, there are powerfully held assumptions that men who choose to work with children are effeminate, homosexual or indeed paedophiles, and consequently these perceptions only serve to discourage both homosexual and heterosexual men to work with children, which of course further impacts the overall numbers of men working in this field. And so by many, men working with young children are viewed at best with caution and at worst with suspicion and unease. Indeed, more than 50% of men surveyed by the London Early Years Foundation said that they would feel discouraged from pursuing a career in the early years sector, the biggest reason being that of societal attitude and the concern that they would be perceived as abusers. This, I would suggest, is the real tragedy of a contemporary society satu-rated with increasingly lurid, disturbing and unravelling stories of child abuse that litter the scandalised post-Savile landscape like hidden IEDs, ready to blow up in men's faces at any moment if they put a foot wrong.

So men's otherwise carefree, playful and caring interactions with children have become contaminated by the fear of being accused of inappropriate behaviour or even targeted as a perpetrator, one consequence being that touch, perhaps the very essence of what it is to be a pro-social, attachment-orientated human, has become something subverted, dangerous, corrupted even. I have heard men say that they would no longer take the hand of a lost child (on the radio recently a man said he would rather roll up a newspaper and get the child to hold on to that instead) or have second thoughts about going to watch their daughter at the Saturday morning gym class because of the accusatory looks of other parents. Many men are becom-ing increasingly inhibited around young children, and of course this translates into the absence of men within a professional context, be it primary school teaching, early-years care work or indeed play therapy.

And what does this also teach children about men? Much is said about the importance of children experiencing positive adult role models, particularly those children who may have experienced high levels of family conflict, their fathers often being either violent or absent. The fact that this absence is mirrored systemi-cally on a wider societal level can only be to the significant detriment of children, becoming part of a wider pattern of children's contact (or lack of contact) with men during their formative, developmental years. According to research by the Children's Workforce Development Council undertaken in 2008, 17% of children from lone-parent families have fewer than two hours a week contact time with a man, while 36% have fewer than six hours, and this raises many questions about the dynamics of gender socialisation and the early powerful messages that chil-dren internalise about the role of men and fathers. If children, boys in particular, are not destined to repeat the 'sins of the father', then I would suggest there needs to be some serious thought applied to how these entrenched patterns of gender division can be addressed.

This inevitably takes us back to attachment theory, where the story of gender identification begins and where the early foundations for children's later patterns of relating are established. What do we mean when we talk about gender identity and gender role, and why is this important when we think of a young child's for-mative early years and this notion of a *positive male role model*, a phrase merrily bandied about in many a workplace and that for many men working in predomi-nantly female teams feels like either a badge of honour (spot the nice man) or a proverbial albatross around the masculine neck?

We can generally think of gender identity as the internalised sense of maleness or femaleness that derives from a combination of many complex influences, for example an identification with parental beliefs, attitudes and expectations, as well as the dynamic interplay between innate biological factors and learned cultural influences. And then there is gender role, more of a cultural construct that emerges from the beliefs, attitudes, expectations and behaviours that may be considered as gender-appropriate within specific cultures. Whilst there are many cross-cultural differences between the roles and expectations of men and women, during infancy it is the mother who remains the primary caregiver. From an attachment perspective the earliest bond, the first relationship, is most likely to be made with the mother, who becomes the primary identification figure for both boys and girls. For girls, this same-sex identification with the mother means that they do not have to adjust in order to consolidate a feminine gender identity and develop a wider sense of maternal identification. For boys of course this is a somewhat different process. In order to begin to form a beginning sense of masculine identity, a boy has to shift his primary identification away from his maternal attachment figure and develop identification with a male figure, usually the father.

This process of early gender identification has powerful, far-reaching implications for both boys and girls who may have grown up in situations of domestic or sexual abuse. The very men with whom they are seeking to identify are frightening, unpredictable, abusive or simply not there. These are the children who are referred into therapy and for whom it is important to experience an alternative version of manhood so that some of the powerful narratives, scripts and stories of childhood can be re-written. The legacy of disturbed attachment is far reaching, and this is why, across the early years in both therapeutic and educational services, the presence of positive male role models is indeed so important, so that children can experience men who are non-abusive and non-threatening.

But whilst there are many professionals and parents who would welcome the difference that men can bring to work with children, there are clearly some major barriers to overcome, barriers which have kept the numbers of men working in the field of child care to around a very lowly 2%. Issues of pay and status also come into the equation, issues which both reinforce institutional sexual discrimination and gender division within our society and also perhaps communicate something about the extent to which we value children (and women for that matter). So how does this translate into the profession of play therapy within the UK? Currently (2014) the number of men registered with the British Association of Play Therapists stands at just a little more than 4%. A demographic survey of Association of Play Therapy members in the United States in 2002 had the number of men a little higher at just ore than 10%, although it should be acknowledged that training and professional routes into the play therapy profession differ considerably in the U.S. Interestingly, but not unsurprisingly, this research also showed that the vast majority of children referred for therapy were boys.

Thinking about this figure within the context of other related professions I can't help but reflect anecdotally upon the journey of my own professional training. During my social work training, men made up close to a third of the overall intake, and when I undertook my training in dramatherapy this dropped to more like one fifth. For my play therapy training I was the solitary male, a pattern that has more or less been consistently maintained over the years in play therapy programmes in the UK, there being typically being either no men or just a single man in training during any given intake. It is an interesting professional trajectory and does I think say something about the gender construction and societal expectation of the respective professions. In a sense, the closer I became to the world of the child the more my minority status as a man has been reinforced.

In relation to training and the choices that people may make, terminology is important. A demographic profile of students entering training with four British Association of Counselling and Psychotherapy (BACP) courses (Coldridge and Mickelborough, 2003) indicated that overall men accounted for 20% of the intake, with some variance between higher- and further-education institutions, and this figure seems to be more or less replicated in terms of undergraduate psychology training across the UK. So men are a well-established minority in respect of the career pathways that may lead them towards, for want of a better word, the 'caring' professions. But this is still a far cry from the 4% of BAPT registered male play therapists or the 2% of men working more generally in the field of early years, and this raises questions around the connotations of the word 'play' and again the stigma that many men may feel when entering a world that is primarily seen as female.

So to generalise, the figures suggest that the profession of play therapy consists of mostly women, working with mostly boys, who have been mostly victims of men. It is an interesting thought and one that both underlines and perpetuates the deeply entrenched gender divisions that dissect our society. It also leads us to the stories about men that get played out within the playroom, powerful echoes and parallels of children's experiences within their families that get enacted within the therapeutic relationship. Lanyado (2003) speaks of the children that we carry around in our pockets, the children who have perhaps evoked a powerful counter-transference response and leave behind an enduring, internalised presence. We carry them in our hearts not pockets, a therapist colleague once said to me recently. But hearts or pockets, these are the children that embody the notion that each therapeutic encounter should leave us changed in some way, both therapist and child.

One such child was William,[1] whose father had died suddenly from a heart attack and who had been referred to our service due to the anger that he was acting out towards his mother. William was just nine years old when his father died, and his mother, acting in a way that she hoped was protective and perhaps through the frosted lens of her own grief, denied William the opportunity to see the body of his father even though he had clearly expressed his desire to do so. She thought that the sight of his father's dead body would be too upsetting for William and sought to shield him from the inevitable distress that would follow. His response, predictably, was one of fear and anger, and the only place these feelings could be located were within his mother, towards whom he hit, kicked, spat and swore.

In his sessions William enacted angry stories about good and bad characters that would fight and kill each other, only to be resurrected and killed again. I was shot many times and magically brought back to life as William sought some sense of control over life and death. At other times we played games and laughed and joked with one another, and the strong paternal counter-transference that I experienced communicated the intensely felt absence of William's own father, whose presence was never that far away.

Some weeks later William asked if he could use the clay that sat in a plastic container underneath the table. 'Sure', I said. 'You can choose whatever you would like to play with in here'. Pulling the container out into the middle of the floor he announced that he was going to make his 'dad', and from the lumpen, inert clay he worked quietly and seriously to fashion a model of his father which he then lay flat on the floor, face up, on a piece of white paper. It wasn't his 'alive dad' William explained; it was his 'dead dad'. William then instructed me to go and stand in the corner of the play room, facing away so that I could not see what was happening in the middle of the room. But although rendered temporarily blind I could hear William as he sat down beside the clay model of his dead father and began to tell him how much he loved him and missed him and wanted him back. It was a powerful and moving moment in which William had created a dramatic, ritualised way to say the things to his father that he had previously been unable to do, to finally say goodbye to him. As is so often the case in play therapy, children will invariably find a way to do what they need to do.

The sensory nature of the clay that facilitated this experience felt deeply meaningful, evocative of the many creation myths from different religions and cultures across the world in which first man or woman is fashioned from the dust, soil and mud of the primitive earth. First man, first father. And it seemed poignant too that I was sent to the corner whilst William did what he so needed to do, as if the momentary presence of two fathers in the room was too paradoxical to entertain, the problem solved through the temporary banishment of the therapist.

This was clearly a pivotal moment in the therapy, and in the following sessions William would occasionally ask me questions about his mother. Had I seen her in the waiting room? What did I think of her? Did I think she looked nice today? I had a sense of where these questions might be leading us and gently acknowledged with William that he seemed to be thinking a lot about how I felt towards his mother. And not long after, the moment arrived. 'So . . . if you like my mum . . . you could marry her couldn't you', said William with a poignant look of hope in his eyes. I felt deeply moved, as the transference and counter-transference so implicit in the work became conscious and tangible, and I struggled for a moment to think how to best respond. 'Ah, I see. So you would like me to marry your mum. So then it would be like you have got your dad back again' (or a new dad, I should have said perhaps). I reflected with William that I was his therapist, not his father, but acknowledged how much he missed him and would like him back. It was as if the symbolic, ritualised farewell to his deceased father that he had enacted previously had created some emotional space for William, allowed him to begin to move on from his paralysing grief and anger to the point where he could entertain space for other father figures in his life. And the emergence of the material into the realm of the conscious allowed us to speak about William's father openly, which in turn enabled conversations to take place between William and his mother, their own relationship enhanced by the process.

It was a poignant and moving encounter, and my experience of working as a male play therapist within the social care sector is often one of polarisation, that within the transference relationship I come to symbolically represent for children either the idealised father figure or the victimising perpetrator. It is a challenging continuum to inhabit and evokes strong counter-transference responses about the relationship with my own father and the stories that I bring to these encounters. My father was a complex man: harsh, critical, periodically depressed and often absent both physically and emotionally. At other times he was engaging and deeply charismatic, and it was not until my early twenties that I began to understand the true nature of his mental health difficulties and could put his behaviour into some kind of meaningful context. I often think I drifted into the world of therapy without much conscious forethought, and most probably this was the case, but on an unconscious level I have little doubt now that this casual (or causal) trajectory was in response to my experiences as a child and most of all my problematic relationship with my father. After all, we are all as therapists driven in powerful ways toward the work we do: the archetypal wounded healer. Physician, heal thyself, as the proverb goes.

And perhaps this is also the answer, or part of the answer, to why I have found myself working within predominantly female-orientated professions: social work, dramatherapy and ultimately play therapy. Over the years and through the course of both personal therapy and clinical supervision I have had cause to reflect upon my own narrative identity, stories of paternal conflict, authority and power and the part that these have played in my developing sense of personal and professional identity. But as I say, I think the relationship with my father is just part of this story. Indeed, it was my mother's influence that nudged me into the 'caring professions', so to speak, and my own experiences as a young child have played a big part in deciding to train in play therapy. It is important I think to reflect upon who and why we are, our blind spots, growing edges and personal stories that we weave and bind together to form some kind of greater whole, albeit a little knotted and ragged at times.

So whilst for William I symbolised something of an idealised father figure, it has not always been the case. Another of the children that I carry Lanyado-like in my ever-burgeoning pocket is Lucy, with whom I worked for many years. Lucy had one of the most traumatic abuse histories of any child I have worked with, a catalogue of entrenched, familial sexual abuse, trauma and neglect that stretched back to her very early years and ultimately led to her move into the care system. In the children's home where she was placed, Lucy stole, hoarded food, soiled and smeared and lay traps on the floor around her bed to alert her to any potential night-time attack. I worked with Lucy over a period of five years, undertaking weekly play therapy sessions in conjunction with support from CAMHS and consultation with her carers. Her interaction with male carers and teaching staff was often sexualised and provocative, most likely a protective strategy on her part, a pattern of relating and expectation that had become deeply embedded over the years of her abuse. For children like Lucy the moment of abuse perhaps came almost as a relief, a certainty preferable to the constant terror of watching, waiting and fearful anticipation.

When Lucy was first referred for therapy it was felt that she would benefit from working with a male therapist, to provide her with an experience of working with a benign, non-abusive figure. With hindsight I wonder about this decision, and whilst in the longer-term I think it was helpful the early period of the work proved to be challenging. She had been abused by both parents in fact and indeed by most adults in her early life, so powerful dynamics were likely to be played out whatever the gender of the therapist. In her sessions Lucy was often chaotic and controlling and sometimes dissociative. Therapeutic limits were critical, and I recall on one occasion during the early, beginning period of her therapy we played a game of catch with a small beanbag. When I wondered aloud about the rules of the game Lucy asked if she had to take her clothes off. I recall feeling shocked and deeply disturbed, and it was as if the very intimacy of the play therapy space felt too overwhelming at times, her core identity being so enmeshed with her experiences of sexual abuse and adult grooming. I recall during my training, Ann Cattanach spoke about how as play therapists we talk to children about playing together, going to a special place, and that we won't tell other people about what it is we do. This is a generalisation of course, but the point is that for children like Lucy the very process of play therapy can contain strong parallels with their own experience of abuse and that we need to be mindful of the things we say and the meaning that might be attributed to our words by the children that we work with.

I had to work hard to establish a sense of safety and trust in our sessions together, including at times acknowledging directly with Lucy her fear that I might hurt or abuse her in the way that men had hurt her before and reasserting myself as a safe, non-abusing man. Lucy played out scenes of neglected, homeless children being shut out of the house by uncaring, wicked mothers. She cooked me porridge for breakfast that I would have to keep on eating until it made me sick, or else it was secretly laced with poison. In her sandplay, houses would quickly become flooded, their foundations collapsing and turning into murky, poisonous swamps where dangerous creatures lurked menacingly. Every symbol of nurture or protection was quickly subverted in one way or another, a powerful portrayal of her own experience of adults that were unpredictable and untrustworthy.

In later sessions, Lucy used dolls to enact graphic scenes of past sexual abuse, and I became the target for her outburst of anger as I momentarily became the perpetrator. '*You did it . . . it was your fault*', she would shout at me, and I would find myself rendered speechless by the power and intensity of her projective energy. I was the man in the room, and Lucy needed somewhere – someone – towards whom she could direct her rage, fear and shame. It was a critical moment in the therapy, for both of us, and manageable only as a result of the length of time that we had worked together and the fact that our relationship was robust enough for Lucy to express her rage and for me to contain it. But saying that, this albeit brief period of the work had a powerful and disturbing personal impact, and I recall that for several nights I experienced distressing dreams about the sessions. Be it projective identification or counter-transference (elements of both I would think), Lucy had displaced those intolerable, toxic parts of herself, leaving me feeling temporarily poisoned to the extent that it seeped into my own unconscious, sleeping state. Projective identification is a powerful if primitive form of both communication and defence which in the context of work with very traumatised, abused children can permeate the very core of the therapeutic process. As Waska (1999: 156) says, "therapists are inevitably touched, contaminated, and seduced by these dynamics. The effects of projective identification are strong and can produce intense countertransference reactions".

And so within this heady projective continuum the male play therapist can oscillate between the positions of idealised father and abhorred perpetrator, expressions of the child's own confusions about these two roles that within the context of their experiences are more often than not inhabited by the same person. For Lucy and myself, it was a test of the resilience of our relationship, and indeed we survived this test and continued to work together for some considerable time. Having outgrown the children's home, Lucy moved to a foster placement and ultimately into supported housing with her elder brother where, now in her early twenties, she still lives. Trauma doesn't go away; like the creases in a crumpled and then unfolded sheet of paper the marks will always remain visible, but for many of these young people life goes on. But the important experience for Lucy, who as a child had no voice, was that of being able to control, direct and pace the process of her therapy and in time find solutions and explore different strategies for coping. And just a word on impact issues: My own capacity to contain and manage the intensity of the work was only made possible through the support of my clinical supervisor and therapist colleagues. This work can leave one feeling depleted and changed, as it should do, but the opportunity to process and explore these feelings is as critical as the therapy itself, indeed is part of the therapy.

Themes of power and authority are never that far away in any discussion about gender and therapy. Many years ago now, during my dramatherapy training, I undertook a placement in a local authority family centre running a group for parents referred by children's services due to a range of social care concerns. Inevitably it was a group of women, mostly single mothers and the majority of them victims of domestic abuse. All were struggling with low incomes and poor housing, difficulties compounded by their experience of a social services organisation that was at best inconsistent and at worst oppressive. I recall feeling uncomfortable in my role as facilitator, once again being the only male in the group, but in this context a role that, by sheer definition, carried echoes of male power and authority that were strongly resonant for the group members. I took these feelings to my supervisor (himself a man) and talked about my feelings of discomfort, that I might get it wrong, make a mistake and hurt or damage the women in the group in some way.

We explored the counter-transference and what this might be communicating about what was happening within the group, and then my supervisor looked me in the eye and told me that I was confusing 'therapist' with 'the rapist'. At the time I thought this was something of a clichéd, perhaps inappropriate comment, and I was unsure what to make of it. To be honest I am still unsure, but I think it was essentially a reflection about power and vulnerability, how power is felt and perceived and the sense of these emotional dynamics being inexorably linked to gender (and sexuality). My fear was that I might somehow harm the women in the group, who had themselves been harmed by men, and intertwined within this was my own personal narrative around paternal power and authority. It is hard to unravel the threads sometimes.

But as a white, middle-class, middle-aged, heterosexual man it is no bad thing to experience being in a minority, although sitting within the warm empathy of the therapeutic community I realise it does not come with the continual prejudice, discrimination, fear (and anger) that many other minority groups experience on a day-to-day basis. It is a choice I have made after all, and as a male therapist, sitting in a room with families who have experienced societal and community prejudice and discrimination in all manner of ways and have had little choice in their lives, I am under no illusion as to the implicit power dynamics in the room, however warm and empathic I hope to be. By sheer virtue of gender, race and class these dynamics will to a certain extent be at play, and to assume otherwise is, I would suggest, in itself an expression of power. When meeting with parents and carers it is important to have these conversations, to explore how it feels working with a male therapist and to gain some sense of the family's and child's narrative in this respect. After all, it is the quality of the relationship with the parents or carer that will ultimately determine the success of the therapeutic intervention with the child.

Another child who always remains with me is Peter, with whom I worked for around two years. Like Lucy, Peter had a history of catastrophic neglect and abuse, and the case notes revealed a disturbing picture of him being treated worse than the family dog, his food left in a bowl in the corner and being kicked and beaten on a regular basis. A single child, he was around seven years old when he was finally made subject to a care order; one can only wonder why it took so long. As a consequence of his severe neglect, Peter presented with considerable developmental delay, both physically and emotionally. His language was poor, his motor control was uncoordinated, he could barely use a knife and fork and he suffered from both enuresis and encopresis. Emotionally, Peter was dysregulated, moving between states of anger, distress, fear and passive withdrawal, and it was powerfully apparent that he had very little experience of a consistent attachment relationship. At the point of his referral to our service, Peter was beginning to make good strides within his foster placement, progress that was in itself symptomatic of all that had been so absent in his early years.

In his sessions, Peter quickly became very regressive and seemed to grow tangibly younger by the week as he crawled around the playroom on all fours, babbled incomprehensively and made little dens for himself in the corner of the room out of cushions and beanbags. I liked Peter and enjoyed working with him, and although the sessions were demanding and often emotionally draining he evoked from within me a strong sense of paternal warmth. When he sat in his den, silent but ever vigilant from behind his rising shield of cushions, I would reflect aloud to myself, a kind of therapeutic mumbling you might say, about how it felt warm and safe in the den and all the things that he might be able to see and hear outside. When he felt ready, Peter would push himself out through the cushions like a kind of birth, a prelude of what was to come. At other times he would sit enveloped by the beanbag and demand to be read stories whilst he noisily sucked water from a bottle.

Peter often liked to play in the large sand tray we had in one corner of the room, although immerse might be a better word. In true embodied fashion, he would throw off his shoes and socks and clamber into the sand tray and marvel at the feel of the cold, gritty sand between his toes as he played at burying his feet. Babbling away to himself, an echo of my own therapeutic mumbling, Peter would lose himself within the dreamy, non-verbal, sensory quality of the sand that itself, like Peter, was barely contained by the boundaries of the sand tray. Watching Peter, I was reminded of Winnicott's (1958) notion of the infant's capacity to play alone, but in the presence of another, the 'resting state' in which the child feels safe enough to creatively explore the environment. Like a dreamy, dissociative reverie, it is a state wherein unrelated, nonsensical and disconnected thoughts can begin to playfully emerge in this magical in-between world. And within the context of this 'maternal reverie' I wondered about the meaning of my own presence as I sat by the side of the sand tray, watching Peter play. Was I mother or father? Or perhaps a symbolically rendered temporary transgender composite of the two?

The sessions progressed in this manner for a while until one week, as I sat once again by the side of the sand tray, Peter suddenly announced 'now you have to borne me'. And so sitting on the corner of the sand tray, my own feet themselves now immersed in the sand, Peter climbed onto my lap and held me around the stomach. With a few guttural gurgles and tiny whimpers he slid down from my stomach and between my legs and was duly 'delivered' into the sand tray – a helpless infant baby. He lay there for a few seconds, curled up in a semi-foetal state, and then gradually opened his eyes, took a little look around and slowly but surely let out the magnificent bellowing first cry of the new-born baby. It was quite a moment in my early play therapy career, itself in its infancy, and certainly the first time I had ever given birth. I felt extremely moved by the experience and once again amazed at the child's capacity to find a way to do what they need to do. Like the clay in William's play described earlier, the deeply regressive and transitional quality of the sand seemed to be a fundamental part of this process for Peter, itself acting as both midwife and archetypal birthing mother. Of course, another consideration for the male play therapist is that of touch. If Peter had been a girl would I have been so permissive in allowing her to climb up onto my lap? Most likely not, and overall I would describe myself as being over-cautious of physical contact when working with children whose bodily boundaries have been so violated in the past.

In the weeks that followed, Peter began to grow up as fast as he had regressed in the period leading up to his 'birth'. He crawled, babbled, toddled and began to speak his first words, drinking hungrily from the bottle before moving on to solids. Essentially, it was a process of re-parenting, his sessions a symbolic echo of the real experience of re-parenting he was getting through his foster placement. And let it be said: a good, nurturing and containing foster placement for a child like Peter is the best possible intervention one could hope for. As a therapist I learned a great deal from Peter: how to trust the process, not to rush things, to simply 'be' and not get too anxious about effecting therapeutic change. Our sessions came to an end when Peter was placed some distance away with long-term foster carers. It was not an easy ending – they invariably never are – but some months later I received a telephone call from his new carers as Peter had asked if I could visit him in his new home. It was not my usual practice as a therapist to make these kinds of follow-up visits or indeed to make home visits at all, but in consultation with my supervisor it seemed both appropriate and important; it felt the right thing to do. So I travelled the several hundred miles to Peter's new home, where we had tea together and later went for walk on the nearby windswept sandy beach. We even played in the sand for a while, an unspoken evocation of times gone by. And then we said goodbye, and I caught the train back home. Peter was happy with his new family, and it was as if a part of him needed me to see them all together, a way of linking and weaving the disparate parts if his life together into some kind of coherent whole. I was happy to see him so settled and I also missed him, which I guess was just as it should be. Sometimes it is simply a privilege to have these children pass through our lives.

The experience of working with a male therapist was I think valuable for Peter, but he would have had an equally valuable (if different) experience of working with a female therapist. What he needed was re-parenting, the opportunity to go back to the beginning and fill in the missing pieces, and he did that both within his therapy and within his foster placement. When he needed me to be a symbolic mother, gender was no obstacle, and that is the power of play therapy – 'in here we can be whatever we choose to be'. For other children therapist gender may be much more of an issue for consideration and indeed should be thought about carefully, for example within the context of the child's parental relationships or perhaps the specific nature of a child's experience of trauma or sexual abuse. Sometimes, of course, there simply may not be the option, which takes us back to the issue of the absence of males across the play therapy profession.

As I say, there are many barriers that I believe prevent more men from training in play therapy, barriers that are mostly to do with perceptions, stigmas, stereotypes, status and perhaps a lack of understanding as to what play therapy really is. It is a young profession after all, and perhaps in time some of these barriers will be broken down. The perceived feminisation of early-years work is clearly an issue, with play therapy occupying a position somewhere towards the thin end of the social care wedge, so to speak. Psychology, social work, teaching and the wider arts therapies are all areas that see, to varying degrees, fewer men in attendance. The opportunities children have for free, unstructured, self-directed play are being eroded enough as it is, colonised by technology, social anxiety, and the national obsession with assessments and targets, and it is a shame then to see children's early developmental experiences further diminished by the entrenched gender divisions within our society that distances men from the child's world. 'We know what we are, but know not what we may be', wept Ophelia as she grieved for her lost father, and indeed it is important that children know what they may be and might become, possibilities shaped by their early, formative play experiences.

As therapists, we are more than adept at exploring issues of power and gender, adroitly able to enter into post-modern, constructivist conversations about (for example) the feminist discourse within psychotherapy and how the dynamics of power and oppression are played out on both familial and wider systemic levels. But much of this discourse is expressed from a therapist perspective and directed towards what we might call, for want of a better word, the 'client population' or indeed the organisation, more often than not held up as the masculine oppressor and rightly so in most circumstances. Let us not kid ourselves where the power lies, however much we might like to think otherwise. What these conversations sometimes miss, or perhaps conveniently circumnavigate, are the issues of gender and power within the therapist community itself. Games around hierarchy and status are played with the utmost seriousness and heavily rule bound by markers like salary or the privileged funding streams that flow, or otherwise, from central government. Where does play therapy stand within the arts therapies? Where do the arts therapies stand within psychotherapy? Where does psychotherapy stand within psychology? And so on. But these are all questions for another day. As a white, middle-class therapist, when I sit on the floor in the playroom with a child or in a consulting room with the child's parents, the presence of power is a palpable, tangible reality. When we talk of children or families who are 'not engaging' we need to ask what it is about us, the therapist, that might be providing obstacles to the relationship.

And so as I arrived for the first day of my play therapy training and sat in the obligatory welcome circle, scanning the faces around me as I took in the fact that I was indeed the only male present, I recall the fleeting sense of feeling like some kind of curio, tangibly aware of the cartoon-like punctuation marks that floated in the air above the group like enquiring thought bubbles in the anticipatory atmosphere of the training room. Question marks, exclamation marks, the conspiratorial parenthesis, enclosed in hushed whispers. In these modern times they might be replaced by little sparkly emoticons that twinkle into existence with a faintly surprised pop: a smile, wink, frown or grimace even. At times I felt like an interloper, as if I didn't belong (the gate crasher at the play therapy party), and often, perhaps in some kind of introjected way, I wondered if I did indeed belong as I hovered on the periphery trying to discover my optimal zone of proximity to the group. Was I in or out? Wanted or unwanted? At other times I felt like a token, the symbolic manifestation of all things male and the veritable voice of mankind. At all times the projective territory of the group process felt both powerful and complex, in the sense of the meaning that my gender must have held for the group and indeed what theirs held for me. After all, as group members we each had our own story about our respective journeys towards a training in play therapy, the particular drives, motivations, fears and desires that propel us along our personal trajectories, many of them no doubt informed by experiences of gender, power and sexuality. I became acutely aware of the respective elements of my own masculine and feminine identity and the extent to which I may have privileged one over the other as I sought to position myself within the overall group identity and indeed those aspects made subject to a process of emotional neutering – to render myself 'safe'. In retrospect, I wished we had been encouraged as a group to reflect more upon this gender dynamic, as it was a significant part of our learning process together.

But as it was, the course progressed, and my fellow group members would occasionally sidle up to me in a quiet moment and ask the question. . .'so what is it like . . . you know . . . being the only man'? It is a question, all these years on, which I still don't quite know the answer to.

Note

1 Names and associated identifying information have been anonymised and disguised to protect confidentiality.

References

Blount, J.M. (2005) *Fit to Teach: Same-Sex Desire, Gender and School Work in the Twentieth Century*. Albany: State University of New York Press.

Cameron, C. (2001) Promise or Problem? A Review of the Men Working in Early Childhood Services. *Gender, Work and Organisation* Vol 8 (4), 430–453.

Cameron, C. & Moss, P. (2004) *Gender Issues in Care Work in Europe*. Thomas Coram Research Unit, Institute of Education, University of London.

Coldridge, L. & Mickelborough, P. (2003) Who's Counting? Access to UK Counsellor Training: A Demographic Profile of Trainees on Four Courses. *Counselling and Psychotherapy Research: Linking Research with Practice* Vol 3 (1), 72–75.

Lanyado, M. (2003) *The Presence of the Therapist*. New York: Routledge.

London Early Years Foundation (2012) *Men Working in Childcare: Does it Matter to Children*. London.

Sargent, P. (2005) The Gendering of Men in Early Childhood Education. *Sex Roles* Vol 52 (3/4), 251–259.

Waska, R.T. (1999) Projective Identification, Countertransference, and the Struggle for Understanding over Acting Out. *The Journal of Psychotherapy Practice and Research* Vol Spring 8 (2), 155–161.

Winnicott, D.W. (1958) *The Maturational Processes and the Facilitating Environment*. London: Karnac Books.

Chapter 4

Bridging the cultural divide

Meeting cultural challenges with enhanced awareness, knowledge and skills

Geraldine Thomas

This chapter identifies and discusses cultural challenges within the practice of play and filial therapy that have emerged in child and family interventions, in mental health settings, and in schools. The term 'culture' here refers to historically transmitted ideas and practices related to race, religion and ethnicity and thus encompasses beliefs, customs, language, thoughts, symbols, values and norms (Kroeber and Kluckhohn, 1952: 181). When defined as 'shared patterns of behaviours, interactions, cognitive constructs and affective understanding that are learned through a process of socialization' (CARLA), culture also influences family structures and parenting styles.

Challenges have arisen from a variety of contexts in which the effects of culture on attachments, child development, family structures and relationships and mental health itself were perceived and recognised by the therapist as potentially affecting the therapeutic progress.

In the writer's practice, direct work with children and young people presented few challenges, as the universal and cross-cultural approach of child-centred play therapy transcended most barriers to knowledge and understanding. However in working collaboratively with parents, cultural taboos about relationships and confidentiality, high mistrust as well as assumed culturally associated feelings of shame hindered the ability to talk about trauma and to explore earlier experiences, therefore limiting understanding of the child's behaviour in the context of these experiences. Described are challenges such as gaining trust, successful communication and overcoming language and cultural barriers, with each requiring enhanced self-awareness, knowledge and skills to consolidate the development of a therapeutic alliance.

Background

Widespread diversity in twenty-first-century Britain often makes culture invisible. For the child it is similarly invisible, as it is inextricably woven, among complex textural variations and subtly hued strands, into the fabric of children's and their families' lives and their experience of being. The child or young person referred for play therapy is above all a troubled child, and the reasons for which referral has been made are considered within developmental, emotional, behavioural and systemic frameworks. Yet many contexts that impact children referred for play therapy and their families are defined by culture. In recognizing the validity of Vygotsky's (1987) views on cultural and historical contributions to development, Bronfenbrenner's theory of social ecology (1979) and cultural influences in the organisation of dyadic attachment (Crittenden and Claussen, 2000), culture's role in the therapeutic process might be viewed as an organising principle of children's behaviour and emotions.

Yet culture is one of the first obstacles to challenge the neutral, non-judgmental stance of the play therapist. Seen through the prism of culture, the play therapy process and the skills employed by the therapist are potentially coloured by bias in observation, expectations, understanding and value judgments of what is 'normative and healthy' development, expected age-related behaviour and developmentally appropriate play. Cultural bias, or blindness, does not only potentially influence the therapist. It may also predispose the client, and the parents who entrust their child to the therapeutic process, to view the therapist with some mistrust and misapprehension. During the referral process information is shared about early experiences and ongoing dynamics; however cultural differences are seldom acknowledged when therapeutic goals are discussed. In responding to the child's play, unfamiliar patterns that arouse curiosity, even alarm, may have been unequivocally accepted had the therapist belonged to, or understood more about, the child's family culture.

Therapists' own experiences of individualist nuclear families may be so distinct from those from collectivist and hierarchically structured cultures that they may be challenged to understand how behaviours and dynamics within these can also constitute a source of strength for others. Conversely, blind acceptance of cultural views or norms may blur the boundaries of what is acceptable and non-acceptable in contrasting value systems and avoid what may negatively influence the child's mental health and development. With relationship patterns deeply rooted in educational and philosophical teaching the play therapist needs to negotiate complex varying standards of environmental or experiential influence. While maintaining unconditional regard for diverse child-rearing beliefs, the therapist must also advocate for the child's right to optimal psychological development.

Culture also predisposes towards variation in how mental health symptoms may be 'constructed'. Some cultural groups may perceive their problems and those of their children to be of a physical or spiritual nature, the result of genetic determination or of 'difference' in relation to the host culture. There may be a strong resistance to acceptance of children's emotional and behavioural difficulties, whether externalising or internalising, as being linked to mental health.

Inter-generationally transmitted cultural patterns of relating (Fonagy, 1999), imported or secondary psychic trauma and a deep mistrust of the values of the host country might contribute to the risks for poor social adjustment and psychological distress. Children in these groups bring unique needs and difficulties related to their culture that require awareness, knowledge and skills such as reactivity to difficulties with acculturation, assimilation, uprooting, language competency, as well as the economic, housing and medical problems which may be expressed in the child's play. Yet cultural stigma associated with seeking professional help and concerns about confidentiality are potential obstacles to therapeutic provision as are histories of trauma and conflict in countries of origin. Additional stressors, such as a high risk of depression among certain ethnic and cultural groups, difficulties in adjusting to new cultural norms, inter-generational conflicts and culturally determined emotions such as shame and guilt in minority and immigrant populations, also require awareness, knowledge and skill.

This chapter examines how the practice of non-directive play therapy, in which the therapist is reflectively responsive to what the child says, does or represents symbolically, remains respectful to cultural meaning by mirroring feelings and affect within the metaphors brought by the child, yet can still be challenged by lack of self-awareness and knowledge of the cultural values expressed within the child's play and in engagement with parents.

This discussion will draw on challenges related to working with three children and families of Afro-Caribbean, Iraqi and Somali origin with a focus on:

1   The bridging of cultural taboo around the concept of mental health
2   Cultural influence on family structures and hostility to host culture
3   Narratives of pain and suffering in the presence of a translator

Each of these will be considered within the context of culturally determined feelings of mistrust and shame as a deterrent to consolidating the therapeutic alliance. The writer's experience of how culture influenced the need for greater competence does not in any way suggest that these expressions of culture are considered stereotypical across the cultural groups discussed.

Each of the cases discussed is based on observation and reflects the therapist's experience of and response to the families' beliefs, values and emotions as they were transmitted during the course of the therapeutic work. None of the concepts that are understood to be culturally determined have been subjected to empirical investigation.

Literature review

Over the past decade cultural considerations in play therapy have been the subject of study and investigation by a number of leading practitioners in the field (Van Fleet and Guerney, 2003; Gil and Drewes, 2005; Schaefer, McCormick and Ohnogi, 2005). The influence of cultural factors on the ways children feel and express themselves through play and the responses of children and parents to culturally specific interventions have been highlighted, as has been the need for cultural competence (Gil and Drewes, 2005; Glover, 2001). Others using family-based interventions have outlined multicultural applications in filial therapy (Van Fleet and Guerney, 2003). Several professionals have emphasised the need to consider how play therapists may need to adjust their approach in order to remain respectful to the child's cultural belief system (Kao and Landreth, 2001) specifically in relation to helping children achieve values, such as self-agency and individualism, which are not always embraced in non-Western cultures. In the field of attachment, the role played by culture in the mother–infant relationship has been extended to a focus on the cultural response to threat and culturally determined self-protective strategies in response to danger (Crittenden and Claussen, 2000).

Within the broader fields of healthcare, psychology and psychotherapy, a large body of research has recently focused on cultural competence theory and practice. Originally conceptualised as cultural responsiveness or sensitivity, cultural competence emphasises the ability to provide care to clients with diverse values, beliefs and behaviours including tailoring delivery to meet patients' social, cultural, and linguistic needs (Betancourt, 2002; Griner and Smith, 2006). Culturally competent care stipulates an assessment of cross-cultural relations and vigilance toward the dynamics that result from cultural differences, expansion of cultural knowledge and adaptation of interventions to meet culturally unique needs (Whaley and Davis, 2007).

With regards to therapist competency, three main areas have been highlighted in the theoretical and empirical literature as being key to positive treatment outcomes: self-awareness, knowledge and skills (Sue, Hall, Zane, Nagayama Hall and Berger, 2009). Whilst the efficacy of enhanced cultural competence is not supported by empirical evidence there can be little doubt that self-awareness, knowledge and skills impact the relationship between therapist and client.

The first of these, the regard for a client as seen through the prism of self-awareness of cultural identity and beliefs, has been shown in psychotherapy to impact clients' perceptions of the therapeutic experience (Ponterotto, Gretchen, Utsey, Rieger and Austin, 2002; Sue and Torino, 2005). Also demonstrated is how awareness of one's values and attitudes is positively associated with how therapists think about and behave with their clients as well as strengthening the therapeutic relationship (Dadlani, 2009).

The second area of competency is that of culture-specific knowledge about diverse populations (Ponterotto and Potere, 2003; Sue and Sue, 2008). Such knowledge integrates culturally competent interventions, including translated, culturally adapted and culturally specific interventions that incorporate the values of the target child, family or group (Gorman and Balter, 1997; Griner and Smith, 2006).

Key issues in culture-specific knowledge are the understanding of the ethnic-cultural differences between the therapist and client, added to which are variations in social class and education that require careful attention to sensitivities related to ethnic background, gender, language preference and fluency, religion and spirituality (Sue, Fujino, Hu, Takeuchi and Zane, 1991; Maramba and Nagayama Hall, 2002). Implicit in having such knowledge may be the therapist's ability to communicate understanding to the client of the presenting problem, an ability to work with racial identity and acculturation and share expectations about treatment goals (Zane et al., 2005; Chang and Berk, 2009).

Skills, together with self-awareness and culture-specific knowledge, complete the three identified variables relating to cultural competence. Examination of cultural influences on the interpersonal skill between the therapist and patient suggests that culture-general relational processes such as empathy, affective involvement, credibility and appropriate disclosure are associated with positive outcomes (Chang and Berk, 2009; Sue and Zane, 1987). Research supporting therapist variables as key in strengthening the therapeutic alliance has shown clients' perceptions of therapist empathy to be associated with multicultural competence as well as demonstrating a relationship between cultural incompetence and treatment dissatisfaction (Fuertes et al., 2006).

The need to understand and work with family risk, when expressed as attachment insecurity, is also impacted by cultural variance. The way in which lack of security challenges families who find themselves separated from their own culture and isolated under conditions of anger, fear and mistrust, may emphasise their diversity in beliefs, histories and religion. Attachment and culture thus inevitably touch on themes of inclusion and exclusion, belonging and alienation, visibility and invisibility and, not least, power and powerlessness (White, 2006).

Culture, attachment practices and child development

In early caregiving and child-rearing contexts, attachment practices that parents believe to be culturally appropriate may conflict with acceptable norms in the new environment. Cultural influences on parenting make different demands on parents, and historical, cultural and ethnic views on parent child interactions and family relationships can blur the boundaries between what is acceptable and what is unacceptable parenting behaviour within accepted cultural norms.

Another fundamental challenge arises from the difference in perspective regarding independence versus interdependence. Cultural attachment variance may emphasise the interdependence of family and community members with family and extended family, with the community playing a critical role in contributing cultural values and practices to the child's development.

Parents' own attachment histories may be predisposed to or have precluded the formation of close bonds or 'attachments' with partners, family, friends and children. Success in forming close, enduring and supportive relationships occurs amongst those with 'secure' attachments, who are more likely to have had loving care in their early years before they were separated and alienated from family and cultural networks. Others have been forced to leave behind family histories of poor parenting and family values that conflict with those of the culture they currently live in.

The shift from secure to insecure attachment can be caused by mistrust, culturally imposed constraints on closeness leading to anxious, avoidant or disorganised functioning, which inhibits the ability to make close supportive bonds and can lead to conflictual or superficial relationships or isolation (Bifulco and Thomas, 2013).

For those with adverse experiences of separations and losses, isolation and alienation, expectations of future relationships become negative and result in poorer ability to make and maintain new relationships. Cultural identity may be further consolidated by avoidant attitudes characterised by mistrust and enforced self-reliance, in particular when cultural feelings of shame or guilt prevent openness, shared communication and closeness. Set within complex cultural contexts, with relationship patterns deeply rooted in historically transmitted values and beliefs, family attachments can challenge the therapist in many ways.

Context

Among the 6.4 million children and young people aged 5 to 19 in the UK, about 20% are from ethno-cultural backgrounds (Department of Health, 2000). In contrast to what is demonstrated in adult population statistics there is no evidence that mental health problems in children are more prevalent if they belong to an ethnic group. However, there is to date insufficient research on the relationship between ethnicity and child mental health, and there is an acknowledged need for further research on the prevalence of child mental health problems versus resilience in minority ethnic groups (Fonagy and Murphy, 2013).

Children are not only affected by their own experiences but also by those adults who care for them. Such adults often report being affected by the experience of victimisation and racial discrimination.

Risk factors and associations specific to children from ethno-cultural groups include being parented by adults who are asylum seekers or refugees, who may continue to experience trauma and marginalisation as a result of leaving their country of origin. Many ethnic minority groups experience social isolation and insecurity that undermines their ability to parent their children and to support their children's healthy development, age-appropriate emotional regulation and social communication.

Children who experience negative parenting, poor-quality relationships and other adversity in early life due to parental insecurity are at particular risk of poor outcomes including mental health problems (Bifulco and Thomas, 2013). Ethnicity data for clients from a Tier 2 Child and Adolescent Mental Health Service (CAMHS) in north-west London demonstrated increased levels of need for non-white clients, 54.8% versus 31.3%, compared to previous years, similar to that of other CAMHS services in the borough with ethnicity characterised by Arab, Asian, Black British- African, Caribbean, and other, mixed white/black African and mixed/white black Caribbean sub-groups. In seeking service provision the main categories of presenting problems were identified as 'emotional and related symptoms', 'family life and relationships' and 'disruptive behaviour' (Ethnicity Data FRP, 2008–2009).

Establishing a therapeutic alliance:
Awareness, knowledge and skills

The qualified play therapist is expected to be trained to a high enough level of competency to apply interpersonal and therapeutic skills with a range of culturally diverse client groups, intervene in a manner that is culturally relevant and also be vigilant to avoid biased or insensitive practice. Skills identified as contributing to heightened cultural competence are integral to an approach guided by the second of Axline's (1989) eight principles; the therapist must accept the child as s/he is so as to enable a child to feel comfortable with him or herself. Most qualified play therapists are also guided by the principle of unconditional positive regard, one of Rogers's (1961) core skills specifying that the therapist suspends any form of personal judgment and accepts the client unconditionally.

Working with a client from an ethno-cultural group that differs from his or her own requires the play therapist to employ both acceptance and unconditional regard alongside increased sensitivity to, or expertise in, cultural orientation. This attitude must be employed throughout, starting with referral meetings, parental introductions, the therapeutic process itself and ongoing reviews. At each step attunement to cultural specificity guides the approach to both child and parents so that judgment does not interfere with either, at all times, feeling accepted for who they are.

Some argue that the mainstream values of psychotherapeutic approaches, in emphasising a perspective focused on client similarities rather than differences, suffice and also that competence itself is less a matter of knowledge and skills than the ability to provide a therapeutic relationship (Bernal and Scharrón-Del-Río, 2001). However, building the therapeutic relationship is a two-way process in which the shared goal is the creation of a mutually satisfying reciprocal relationship that is built on a strong foundation of trust.

The therapist brings to this process shared goals for the child and for the family. In turn children and parents bring a commitment to work collaboratively and to share with the therapist all areas of the child's history, development, family trauma and parenting styles. A shared belief in this process, by both the therapist and client, is considered to have impact on therapeutic outcomes. Yet many cultures have explicit or implicit taboos about relationships and disclosure.

When engaging children in the therapeutic process there is a fundamental understanding that in addition to the relationship between therapist and client, a relationship between the therapist and parent, carer and the wider family system is critical in making the child available for change. The child's psychological change outside the familial environment may challenge the family's ability to assimilate and sustain such change. The openness to change and insight into what cultural resistance to change may be encountered starts with the assessment process.

The child, together with parents or carers, is offered a therapeutic relationship or alliance with the play therapist focused on reducing the child's difficulties and helping the adults in the child's life prevent future problems and to develop an increased understanding of their children's feelings, motivations and needs and thereby improve the family's coping abilities.

For the child the potential clash between what is culturally comfortable and what may feel alien in therapy, in contrast to the more culture-specific language and communication needs of adults, may be moderated by the heavy reliance on nonverbal emotional expression offered in child-centred play therapy. Awareness is required of the need to communicate the child's need for therapy in a manner that is respectful of the culturally determined parental understanding of psychological intervention. Knowledge of the specific cultural constraints on sharing thoughts and emotions with an outsider further guide the application of enhanced skills across each of these domains to contribute to the successful outcome of the child's therapy.

Introductory meeting and assessment

As play is the child's universal language assessment can be undertaken with the child without challenging language limitations. However, when referral information is obtained from parents or carers limitations in comprehension can be the first sensitive area requiring awareness, knowledge and skill so as to communicate the need for referral or service provision without challenging cultural defences. The play therapist should be aware of what is considered normal behaviour according to the client's relevant culture and consider what flexibility there might be for understanding the child's behaviour in new ways. In doing so, awareness of communication styles and knowledge of cultural taboos requires skilful probing with sensitivity to the life contexts that contribute to their children's difficulties.

The first challenge: Making the case for intervention and conveying understanding of culturally defined constructions of mental health

In my first meeting with the mother of C, a young boy of Somali origin referred for a history of 'selective mutism', I was aware of the cultural obstacles to sharing family difficulties outside the immediate family. Knowledge that cultural constraints on sharing for this family were rooted in the perception of psychological vulnerability, as well as that seeking help for emotional difficulties and other mental health–related issues was shameful, prepared me for the resistance I encountered in this meeting. The community to which this young mother belonged encouraged dealing with emotional distress within the family. Family members rather than outsiders and professionals were deemed to have a duty to care for a vulnerable or poorly functioning family member of the community.

C's mother insisted that the family's network was adequately able to cope with her child's mental health needs, and it was evident that her attitude was underpinned by suspicion that any information relating to her child might be shared with others. My empathy for her began by acknowledging my awareness of how difficult it was for her to have to speak to me when her cultural environment dictated that personal problems should not be shared outside the immediate family. I shared my perception that her ambivalence about accepting psychological therapy for her child came from her belief that having a child that was in need of outside intervention would bring shame upon her family. I also empathised that wider knowledge of this amongst members of her community, which espoused collectivist values, would meet with disapproval.

Whereas my knowledge had prepared me for constraints on acknowledging something that was perceived as shameful, and sharing relevant information, my skills emphasised a need to remain sensitive to my role as an outsider. The need to gradually build trust with a family that was resistant to sharing even the most basic of information relating to early adversity, losses or trauma with a therapist who represented values and belief systems that were likely not to be respectful of theirs would be the cornerstone of our future relationship.

The assessment process would require time, and I had no expectation of being given consent to work with this child until I had gained his mother's trust. It was necessary to reassure her that in engaging her son in therapy, I would not challenge her beliefs about child rearing and family life. She clearly communicated the need to have her values, and those of her community, respected. C's mother shared her view that her son's condition was determined by family genetics and that muteness, among children and young men, was not uncommon in her culture of origin.

In addition to reliance on family members and friends and a fundamental mistrust of outsiders, C's mother's poor command of English presented a further challenge. My confidence in my ability to sensitively acknowledge acceptance and understanding without adequate verbal communication and the implications this had for building a strong parent–therapist relationship were further challenged by the knowledge that an interpreter as an additional outsider would not be welcomed.

Given the importance of family members in minority and immigrant populations and specifically my understanding of Somali society as hierarchical with a high respect for elders and shared care of children between family and friends, I considered using a family systems approach in treatment. However, I was also aware of the difficulty of including the wider family in psychological therapy, which might be considered shameful. A further challenge was my understanding of the cultural variation in elicitors of shame, a self-conscious emotion "associated with being negatively evaluated by the self or others, because standards regarding what is good, right, appropriate and desirable have been failed" (Lewis, 1974).

Fear of being negatively evaluated as a mother by others if her child did not speak were exacerbated by Somali cultural beliefs around mental health as polarised between 'sane' and 'insane'. Awareness of this informed my skills to empathically convey to C's mother my understanding of her discomfort that I, among others, might see C's difficulties as something stigmatising and incurable rather than a silent expression of anxiety and need. Because fear of exposure of one's or of the family's 'defective' self is associated with the view of self in terms of others' thoughts and feelings, emphasising the confidentiality of the work was a key, if not critical, recognition of cultural shame associated with vulnerability and behaviour.

C's mother agreed to my offer of eight initial sessions so that I could make an assessment of his longer-term needs, but I also knew that many details of his early care, family stresses or possible traumatic life events had not been shared with me. I felt, like C, that the silence that was imposed on his mother was now also imposed on me.

Following the eight sessions, C's engagement in play therapy was slow. He was initially guarded, uncertain about whether it was safe to trust me, but gradually revealed all his life experiences through play thus obviating the need to verbally disclose all that he had experienced and witnessed. The undirected and developmentally sensitive approach that guides non-directive play therapy gave C permission to make his intra-psychic difficulties rather than his muteness the centrepiece of the work without challenging his need for control. In offering C a chance to speak with his own uncensored language of play the message was conveyed that I was able to accept his language of silence, thus initiating a shift in the power imbalance of his experience of adult–child relationships and laying the foundation for trust.

The choice of play rather than speech as a medium through which C could resolve intra-psychic conflicts, work through trauma and achieve mastery meant that C could work at a symbolic level without mobilising defences to protect against the anxiety of accidental verbal disclosure. In the playroom, C's symbolic enactments transcended all barriers imposed on his speech. Following an 18-month weekly intervention, C was able to freely communicate in the classroom, with peers and with me. I discovered a witty sense of humour and a warmly engaging child hungry for a close and trusting relationship. Importantly, a healthy developmental trajectory with an age-appropriate task focused on relationship building with peers and with others could be resumed.

Second challenge: Attuning to culturally significant play communications in relation to family structure, isolation and hostility

Like many of the vulnerable children referred for play or filial therapy who are the offspring of immigrants who have recently arrived in the UK, G, a 10-year-old boy, and his family had recently arrived from one of the British Caribbean islands.

Regardless of the universality of the language of play, attunement to the child's symbolic and thematic expression of culture at a subtle or directly expressed level is a required skill. Cultural identity or resistance to cultural norms may be expressed as specific thematic content or as music, dance, language, hierarchical systems and family dynamics. Expressions of feelings of difference or relatedness to the cultural norms of the wider system may be communicated in ways that the therapist may have little awareness of.

As play is the symbolic and directly expressed sensorimotor as well as the inter- and intra-personal language used by children, the trained play therapist who is able to connect with the child's deepest emotional expressions may, in responding to core feelings and emotions, be able to bypass knowledge of ethno-cultural differences. Reflection of the child's feelings along with empathy and unconditional positive regard contribute to conditions that facilitate a relationship based on trust, acceptance and understanding. Nevertheless, deeper understanding of the thematic content of the child's play, which is likely to include multiple references to culturally determined family structures, gender roles, dynamics and practice, requires knowledge of ethno-cultural variations.

G was referred to me for play therapy due to difficulty with impulse control, heightened emotional responses when told off, a limited capacity for concentration, need for immediate attention and difficulty in sharing attention with others as well as anxiety and angry and aggressive outbursts in the playground.

Before meeting with the referrer and G's mother to discuss the concerns about his poor behaviour at school I needed to acquire knowledge about his culture. The literature emphasised the diversity of Caribbean families, but a shared statistic for children living in the UK was that only one in five were living with two Caribbean parents. With many Caribbean families having a matrifocal or matricentric structure, 30% of children were raised exclusively by their mothers (Powell, 1986). In Grenada, where C was born and spent his early years, this was 45.3% (Massiah, 1982).

Mrs A reported no difficulties at home with G's behaviour but acknowledged occasional emotional and angry outbursts at home which he found difficult to control. She also spoke of his exceptional cleaning skills and his usefulness in the home and that he performed housekeeping duties much better than his sisters did. G's mother shared his experience of a number of adverse and traumatic events in his early life. His father and his grandmother both died shortly before his family, including four older siblings in their twenties, had left the Caribbean island where he had grown up. Immediately following their arrival in the UK, G's mother had taken on work with a demanding schedule as well as attending university to gain a degree, thus leaving G predominantly to care for himself.

Each of these events was sufficient to cause emotional and behavioural reactions, and I believed these to be compounded by G being the youngest child in a family of adults where little priority could be given to the emotional needs of a much younger child. Although G lived with his mother and his three older siblings, Mrs A's heavy work schedule and studies, which she had taken on to help her better integrate into UK work culture, prevented her from being physically or emotionally available to a child who was also adjusting to a new country and way of life. Spending much time by himself meant that emotionally challenging situations had to be processed without the support or containment from adults such a young boy requires.

I started work with G at the beginning of the school year, and it did not take long for themes of alienation and cultural mistrust to be played out. Within minutes of entering the playroom for the first time he forcefully swung a sword to symbolically sever the imaginary limbs of the bop bag before beheading him. As I reflected the harshness of this treatment G responded that 'this is how people were punished in England…their heads are chopped off …and their faces put on poles'. Alongside repeated demonstrations of English punishments, themes of self-care and needing to be useful in the playroom, G repeatedly apologised for the slightest error and did not dare explore a new interest without permission. Feelings of being unworthy of care, anger at having to feel badly about what he did or felt, as well as attendant feelings of enforced submission and powerlessness dominated his play.

Once G felt safe enough in his sessions to communicate aspects of his life that truly troubled him he engaged in role play that revealed the family dynamics and structures I had hypothesised. My knowledge of the high levels of parental stress experienced by many immigrant Afro-Caribbean families and how this was often associated with shouting, quarrelling and at times also physical punishment in the home was corroborated by G's play themes of conflict, victimisation and powerlessness. In addition G spoke about being left alone in the home, his loneliness, despair and isolation experienced even when his older siblings were close by. Self-awareness cautioned me not to make assumptions about the meaning of G's family structure and the quality of his mother's parenting. I needed to be sensitive not to impute neglect when this could be a culturally accepted norm that implied restricted interaction between parent and child and which had been established long before arriving in the UK. With G's mother having to survive in her new culture with long hours of work I could not easily challenge her strategy for survival.

G's mother attended all the progress meetings offered but initially had difficulty in understanding G's strong need for a primary attachment figure. Acknowledging that she could no longer rely on the help of family and friends to share her care of him she reiterated her cultural expectation that children needed to work to be useful. In the Caribbean they would look after the goats, and now, in a more urban context, G's usefulness would have to be channelled through housework.

In addition to being aware that children were expected to help with domestic chores around the house and that boys were also expected to take care of the yard and run errands (Evans and Davies, 1997), knowledge related to children being required to be obedient, respectful and submissive to their parents informed the skills I needed to apply when Mrs A reiterated her view that she could not accept that children had a right to decisions. For example, the drama classes G was reluctant to attend had been paid for and would be attended whether he enjoyed them or not.

With knowledge and understanding of the many obstacles Mrs A faced, not least in having to apply her culturally determined family structure into a new context, I needed to skilfully translate G's thematic play about marginalisation and the UK as a place of cruel punishment in a way that would be tolerable. The obvious parallels between G's feelings of loneliness and needing to fight for what he needed and those of his mother's were potentially too painful for her to hear. An even greater need for skill was required to address the threat of cultural doom that hung over G's therapeutic progress. Mrs A was aware of an increased association of young Afro-Caribbean men with gun crime and gang culture, and I had gleaned in G's first session a deep mistrust of British culture that pervaded G's family's beliefs. Mrs A shared her conviction that being black in Britain meant being stopped and searched. Awareness of the same association between young Afro-Caribbean men and crime informed my empathy for Mrs A's belief that the UK was a dangerous place for young black boys and implied arrest and victimisation. Her bleak vision of the future corroborated G's view that life for children was without hope and implied failure and annihilation.

Empathy and unconditional positive regard were informed by my awareness of Mrs A's feelings of alienation in having to negotiate her family's transition in the absence of support. Over the course of many reviews she was able to accept that her fears and high mistrust would prevent G from trusting that there was a future for him in the culture into which he had been transferred. In the playroom he had clearly communicated the anticipation of punishment and harsh treatment in England, and only his mother's belief in the possibility of belonging and successful assimilation could free G from the dread of impending failure and punishment.

Filial therapy with an Iraqi family: Negotiating exclusion from a narrative of pain and suffering

In some cases a minimum requirement for culturally competent intervention may be the need for a translated, culturally adapted and culturally specific intervention. Poor cross-cultural communication between service providers and clients due to language constraints is likely to limit constructive exchanges and the building of trust.

No matter how able the therapist is to communicate with clients in a culturally acceptable and appropriate manner, when the client's limited English hampers their ability to benefit from treatment, additional resources are required for therapy to be made accessible. In order to undertake filial therapy with a refugee family from Iraq, an on-site interpreter needed to be made available to engage with the family who had limited English proficiency.

The referral was complex and requested therapeutic service for J, a 9-year-old girl whose family, who had fled Iraq after the 2003 invasion, had already been offered extensive input from adult as well as child and adolescent mental health services. They now lived in a tightly knit community of Middle Eastern refugees in London and each of the children exhibited problematic behaviours which were understood to be associated with trauma, alienation and parental stress and depression.

All members of the family except the father had previous involvement with professionals. Earlier intervention had sought to address the mother's depression and behavioural and emotional difficulties in the children, but it was J who, timid and withdrawn, internalised the family's difficulties. An intelligent and insightful young girl, J sought out her mother's company and hankered for her affection but was rebuffed as her mother struggled to show her any loving feelings. She attributed this to postnatal depression, which she had suffered following J's birth and that had interfered with their bonding process. Unaware of her identification with her daughter she also projected her own un-lovability and experience of familial rejection onto her.

In trying to gain access to her mother J would escalate her attention-seeking behaviour, but instead of the wished-for closeness she achieved a strained relationship characterised by negativity, resentment and bad feelings. She lashed out at her siblings who effortlessly achieved closeness with their mother. By the time I met J her outwardly indifferent demeanour belied somatic symptoms including mobility problems and severe leg pain so that she often had to be carried to her bath or bed.

Important information about the family's past experiences included J's mother's history of being raised by an aunt, a marriage she had reluctantly entered into and a history of family rejection. The themes of hurt and rejection were compounded by a family narrative of brokenness and illness. J's father had been tortured and, while there was no discernible evidence of post-traumatic stress, the humiliation of being disabled and unemployed in a country that did not know or value his previous achievements cast a dark shadow over the family's fragmented identity.

Knowledge acquired informed me that many refugees had been tortured, had experienced violence or had witnessed the killings of friends and loved ones. I also knew that many reported suffering from depression, anxiety and post-traumatic stress disorder, with depression being the predominant diagnosis (Ziegahn et al., 2013). On-going stressors were likely to also include lack of economic resources and loss of identity resulting from change in social status and living standards.

Awareness of potentially high levels of mistrust around confidentiality and heightened feelings of fear and rejection, understanding of what would be tolerable in terms of a stranger in the form of a translator and what stigma might be associated with the provision of a mental health service for the family unit was critical. Referral information had included many adverse experiences including those with the extended family, and I anticipated that building trust would be a major challenge. An explicit contract of confidentiality extended to the interpreter would be critical to the establishment of the therapeutic alliance.

Important knowledge included awareness that the concept of 'mental health' was problematic for many Iraqi people. In Iraq mental health implied severe illness requiring psychiatric treatment, and the need for mental health intervention was highly stigmatising and associated with incurable illness. Instead family and friends were relied on for help. Further awareness of the need to acknowledge symptoms such as crying or bodily aches in preference to using recognised mental health terminology such as depression helped me develop skills that would contribute to the client being more receptive to treatment. Careful structuring of the various stages of filial therapy was required to ensure that the whole family would feel able to participate and, in order to minimise the mental health credentials of filial therapy, the playful and relationship-building qualities of this approach were emphasised.

I structured the sessions so that the parents and I would be the only ones to be present in the room when they played with their child. At the end of the hour, with both sessions completed, we were joined by the Arabic-speaking psychologist so that each parent could process their feelings about what had occurred and their reactions to the session in their own language and that these would then be translated for my benefit.

In our first meeting, accompanied by the Arabic-speaking psychologist, I became aware that each session needed to start with an exchange of pleasantries and small talk before we could progress to our usual discussions and that this would be critical to the success of the rapport-building phase. Acknowledging awareness that J's father had previously been a highly regarded professional whose current unemployment and change in socio-economic standing contributed to the already considerable stress experienced by the family was another building block of the trust we would have to establish before the family work could begin.

Following the play session in which I had demonstrated and modelled the non-directive nature of the sessions I became aware of a palpable anxiety about the permissiveness I had offered J. Both parents worried that this would compromise the climate of obedience and respect that was dictated by their cultural values and that my message that she could do 'almost' anything in this time threatened their belief that a child should be loyal, obedient and not question authority. Careful explanation of their ultimate authority and control in the playroom through employing the limit-setting skill made the unaccustomed permissiveness acceptable, and no other adjustments were required.

Mr and Mrs L needed to be listened to above all, and once each embarked on communicating their reaction to the sessions with the translator, it was difficult for me to interrupt the flood of pain and torment in a language from which I was barred. Once it was translated, I understood that they related their narratives of victimisation and brokenness to the Arabic-speaking translator in their shared language, and it was with her that the trust and confidence were being built. Shame about not loving her daughter as she did her other children and ambivalent feelings about her family, were not felt to be shareable with me. Nor was her narrative of pain and illness to protect against evil, as her collectivist belief that my actions or judgment would further induce feelings of shame prevented full disclosure of the intergenerational rejection and shame that accompanied it. It was this narrative that dominated our sessions and initially interfered with shifting Mrs L's attention to the intimacy J relished when she and her mother smiled and joked together as they rolled Play-Doh into colourful crescent-shaped 'pastries' and other playfully created foods from their shared wider and family culture.

Over the course of six months Mrs J's narrative of brokenness and hurt subsided sufficiently for her to share my awareness of the pleasure and intimacy she and her daughter experienced when together in the playroom. The balance was shifting, J's 'inability' to walk decreased gradually, her dependent infantile need to be carried was replaced by age-appropriate comfort and proximity seeking and her two siblings now demanded their own place in the newly emotionally reconfigured family.

Conclusion

The integrated patterns of beliefs and behaviours that are shared among adults and also children including thoughts, roles and relationships, values, practices and communication all influence what the child and the family bring to the process of play and filial therapy.

In child-centred play therapy the child's spontaneous play may communicate culture related thoughts and feelings and can enable the child to work through conflicts and tensions in cultural experience without relying on verbal expressions. With or without language the child is able to express feelings and perceptions of cultural roles, relationships and practices in relation to new experiences and develop new perspectives on his world.

Communication by the child is thus conducted at a level that is determined by the child or young person and is understood and accepted by the therapist. Such understanding inevitably requires a 'translation' of the language of play used by the child. At times such translation may be challenged by the impenetrable nature or obscurity of play themes and may prevent full comprehension of the child's deepest preoccupations. However, because the child also works through and resolves his difficulties at a symbolic level, the therapist's verbal or non-verbal communication of acceptance suffices.

Such challenges are more often encountered in work with parents or carers and the child's wider cultural network as the families, communities and wider systems that the child is part of each bring with them histories of adversity and experience. This may include practices that are acceptable in the culture in which the child is raised but that are seen as outside accepted norms in childcare practice and current mental health provision. The work undertaken was accepted and approached from the perspective that many of these challenges are brought by the conditions that bring children and their families to live in a culture that is mistrusted by them and that smooth adaptation to the new environment is often hampered by the anger, fear and need that characterises the attitudes of those seeking a place in the new community. Many immigrant or refugee families thus find themselves at variance with the cultural values embedded in British culture. Such variance is magnified when mental health needs are identified and parental shame, implicit in many collectivist cultures, precludes the sharing of confidential material related to caregiving, culture, family structures, history or trauma.

Self-awareness, knowledge and skills, as well as the recognition and acceptance of collectivist cultural shame in response to the need for treatment, contribute to bridging the cultural divide between therapist and client and enable positive outcomes for the child. Each of these skills ultimately contributes to enhanced sensitivity to the adults supporting the therapeutic work with the child and therefore also to the consolidation of the therapeutic alliance.

References

Axline, V. (1989) *Play Therapy*. Boston: Houghton Mifflin.

Bernal, G. & Scharrón-Del-Río, M. R. (2001) Are Empirically Supported Treatments Valid for Ethnic Minorities? Toward an Alternative Approach for Treatment Research. *Cultural Diversity and Ethnic Minority Psychology* Vol. 7 (4), 328–342.

Betancourt, J. R. (2002) *Cultural Competence in Healthcare*: *Emerging Frameworks and Practical Approaches*. The Commonwealth Fund Field Report 2002. Available at www.cmwf.org.

Bifulco, A. & Thomas, G. (2013) *Understanding Adult Attachment in Family Relationships, Research, Assessment, Intervention*. New York: Routledge.

Bronfenbrenner, U. (1979) *The Ecology of Human Development: Experiments by Nature and Design*. Cambridge, MA: Harvard University Press.

CARLA, Center for Advanced Research on Language Acquisition, The University of Minnesota. Available at http://www.carla.umn.edu/culture/definitions.html.

Chang, D. F. & Berk, A. (2009) Making Cross-Racial Therapy Work: A Phenomenological Study of Clients Experiences of Cross-Racial Therapy. *Journal of Counseling Psychology* Vol 56 (4), 521–536.

Crittenden, P. M. & Claussen, A. H. (eds) (2000) *The Organization of Attachment Relationships: Maturation, Culture, and Context*. New York: Cambridge University Press.

Dadlani, M. B. (2009) *Countertransference Behavior and Alliance Quality as a Function of Therapist Self-Insight*. Paper presented at the Northeast regional meeting of the North American Society for Psychotherapy Research. University of Massachusetts, Amherst, MA.

Department of Health (DoH). (2000) *Framework for the Assessment of Children in Need and their Families. Quality Protects*. London: The Stationary Office, Department of Health.

Evans, H. & Davies, R. (1997) Overview of Issues in Childhood Socialization in the Caribbean. In: Roopnarine, J. & Brown, J. (eds) *Caribbean Families: Diversity among Ethnic Groups*: 1–24. Greenwich, CT: Ablex Publishing.

Fonagy, P. (1999), *Transgenerational Consistencies of Attachment: A New Theory*. Paper presented to the Developmental and Psychoanalytic Discussion Group at the meeting of the American Psychoanalytic Association, Washington, DC.

Fonagy, P. & Murphy, M. (2013) *Our Children Deserve Better: Prevention Pays*. Annual Report of the Chief Medical Officer 2012. Department of Health. Available at https://www.gov.uk/government/organisations/department-of-health.

Fuertes, J. N., Stracuzzi, T. I., Bennett, J., Scheinholtz, J., Mislowack, A., Hersh, M., et al. (2006) Therapist Multicultural Competency: A Study of Therapy Dyads. *Psychotherapy: Theory, Research, Practice, Training* Vol 43 (4), 480–490.

Gil, E. & Drewes, A. (eds) (2005) *Cultural Issues in Play Therapy*. New York: The Guildford Press.

Glover, G. J. (2001) Cultural Considerations in Play Therapy. In: Landreth, G. L. (ed) *Innovations in Play Therapy. Issues, Process, and Special Populations* (pp. 31–42). Philadelphia: Brunner-Routledge.

Gorman, J. C. & Balter, L. (1997) Culturally Sensitive Parent Education: A Critical Review of Quantitative Research. *Review of Educational Research* Vol 67 (3), 339–369.

Griner, D. & Smith, T. B. (2006) Culturally Adapted Mental Health Interventions: A Meta-Analytic Review. *Psychotherapy: Theory, Research, Practice, Training* Vol 43, 531–548.

Kao, S.-C. & Landreth G. L. (2001) Play Therapy with Chinese Children. In: Landreth, G. L. (ed) *Innovations in Play Therapy. Issues, Process, and Special Populations* (pp. 43–50). Philadelphia: Brunner-Routledge.

Kroeber, A. L. & Kluckhohn, C. (1952) *Culture: A Critical Review of Concepts and Definitions.* New York: Meridian Books.

Lewis, H. B. (1974) *Shame and Guilt in Neurosis.* New York: International Universities Press.

Maramba, G. & Nagayama Hall, G. (2002) Meta-Analyses of Ethnic Match as a Predictor of Dropout, Utilization, and Level of Functioning. *Cultural Diversity and Ethnic Minority Psychology* Vol 8 (3), 290–297.

Massiah, J. (1982) Women Who Head Households. In: Massiah, J. (ed) *Women and the Family* (pp. 9–69). Cave Hill, Barbados: Institute of Social Economic Policy.

Ponterotto, J. & Potere, J. (2003) The Multicultural Counseling Knowledge and Awareness Scale (MCKAS): Validity, Reliability, and User Guidelines. In: Pope-Davis, D. (ed) *Handbook of Multicultural Competencies: In Counseling & Psychology* (pp. 137–153). Thousand Oaks, CA: Sage Publications, Inc.

Ponterotto, J. G., Gretchen, D., Utsey, S. O., Rieger, B. P. & Austin, R. (2002) A Revision of the Multicultural Counseling Awareness Scale. *Journal of Multicultural Counseling and Development* Vol 30, 153–180.

Powell, D. (1986) Caribbean Women and Their Response to Familial Experiences. In: Massiah, J. (ed) *Women in the Caribbean Part 1* (pp. 83–130). Lewis Institute of Social and Economic Studies, University of the West Indies.

Rogers, C. (1961) *On Becoming a Person: A Therapist's View of Psychotherapy.* London: Constable.

Schaefer, C., McCormick, J. & Ohnogi, A. (2005) *International Handbook of Play Therapy: Advances in Assessment, Theory, Research and Practice.* Lanham, MD: Jason Aronson.

Sue, D. W. & Sue, D. (2008) *Counseling the Culturally Diverse: Theory and Practice* (5th ed.). Hoboken, NJ: John Wiley & Sons Inc.

Sue, D. W. & Torino, G. C. (2005) Racial-Cultural Competence: Awareness, Knowledge, and Skills. In: Carter, R. T. (ed) *Handbook of Racial-Cultural Psychology and Counseling: Training and Practice* (pp. 3–18). Hoboken: John Wiley & Sons Inc.

Sue, S., Fujino, D., Hu, L., Takeuchi, D. & Zane, N. (1991) Community Mental Health Services for Ethnic Minority Groups: A Test of the Cultural Responsiveness Hypothesis. *Journal of Consulting and Clinical Psychology* Vol 59 (4), 533–540.

Sue, S. & Zane, N. (1987) The Role of Culture and Cultural Techniques in Psychotherapy: A Critique and Reformulation. *American Psychologist* Vol 42 (1), 37–45.

Sue, S., Zane, N., Hall, N., G. C. & Berger, L. (2009) The Case for Cultural Competency in Psychotherapeutic Interventions. *Annual Review of Psychology* Vol 60, 525–548.

Van Fleet, R. & Guerney, L. (eds) (2003) *Casebook of Filial Therapy.* Boiling Springs, PA: Play Therapy Press.

Vygotsky, L. S. (1987) *The Collected Works of L. S. Vygotsky.* R. W. Rieber & A. S. Carlton (eds) and Minick, N. (trans). New York: Plenum Press.

Whaley, A. & Davis, K. (2007) Cultural Competence and Evidence-Based Practice in Mental Health Services: A Complementary Perspective. *American Psychologist* Vol 62, 563–574.

White, K. (ed) (2006) *Unmasking Race, Culture, and Attachment in the Psychoanalytic Space*. London: Karnac Books.

Zane, N., Sue, S., Chang, J., Huang, L., Huang, J., Lowe, S., et al. (2005) Beyond Ethnic Match: Effects of Client–Therapist Cognitive Match in Problem Perception, Coping Orientation, and Therapy Goals on Treatment Outcomes. *Journal of Community Psychology* Vol 33 (5), 569–585.

Ziegahn, L., Ibrahim, S., al-Ansari, B., Mahmood, M., Tawffeq, R., Mughir, M., Hassan, N., DeBondt, D., Mendez, L., Maynes, E., Aguilar-Gaxiola, S. & Xiong, G. (2013) *The Mental and Physical Health of Recent Iraqi Refugees in Sacramento, California*. UC Davis Clinical and Translational Science Center. Sacramento: CA: UC Davis.

Chapter 5

Stuck in the dollhouse

A brain-based perspective of post-traumatic play

Natalie Prichard

A small five-year-old girl with untamed curls and startling blue eyes unwittingly introduced me to the potential danger of post-traumatic play and the need for play therapists to have an understanding of the impact of overwhelmingly frightening experiences on a child's developing brain and nervous system. Jay, the youngest of three children, had been removed from the care of her birth parents and referred for therapy due to experiences of abuse and neglect, including family violence.[1] Just minutes into her first play therapy session Jay sat in front of the dollhouse and commenced a sequence of intense and repetitive play without narration. Jay sat transfixed as she banged the adult dolls up and down the stairs and upturned furniture in search of hidden baby dolls. This was followed by more banging, upturned furniture, hiding, searching and banging. While there was movement of the dolls in her play, Jay's body was rigid, her affect flat and her breath still. She made no vocalisation in what appeared to be a re-enactment of family violence; Jay seemed caught in the past and oblivious to my presence. There was no relief or joy in her play. It was a sombre walk as I followed a small slumped form out of the playroom at the end of our session. For several weeks following Jay gave a wide berth to the dollhouse. It was not a safe place to play.

In retrospect, it could be maintained that Jay was re-living elements of her past trauma in her present play, psychologically and physiologically. In playing out her traumatic past in her initial session, Jay inadvertently triggered the same fear response that was present at the time of the original traumas, causing her to become overwhelmed and stuck in her play. Early attachment relationships are crucial in shaping the brain and helping children learn how to manage stress and fear. Developmental trauma, which encompasses interpersonal trauma, abuse and neglect within the early caregiver relationship, has long been observed to wound a child's social, emotional, cognitive and behavioural development (van der Kolk, 2005). Recent decades of research have established that developmental trauma can forge lasting changes to the physiology and structure of the brain, especially the mechanisms involved in regulating stress (Perry, 2009). Child-centred play therapy operates from the Rogerian principal that individuals have an innate trajectory towards healing and growth, given the right conditions. The challenge for present-day play therapists is to examine how emerging insights into the impact of trauma on the brain should inform our practice and how we create the right conditions for healing and growth, both psychologically and physiologically, when working with children and trauma.

Childhood trauma and the developing brain

The play, art and expressive therapies are increasingly recognised as approaches through which traumatic experiences stored in the body and mind can be accessed and integrated (Steele and Malchiodi, 2012). Badenoch affirms that child-centred play therapy "seems an excellent match for what we are learning from neuroscientists about how children's brains and minds get hurt and heal" (2008: 300), although play therapists should also be trauma informed, practising with a theoretical understanding of the psychological and physiological impact of trauma on the developing child. An understanding of trauma theory is advocated by Rothschild (2000) as the most effective means for guarding against the dangers of conducting therapy with traumatised clients. An understanding of how the brain develops and changes is also useful for therapists since it's the brain that processes both traumatic and therapeutic experiences, with therapy ultimately aiming to positively influence the physiology and architecture of the brain (Perry, 2006).

There are several principles of neurodevelopment that are relevant to the treatment of childhood trauma. First, the brain is organised in a *hierarchical* manner and develops in a *sequential* fashion from the lower sensorimotor areas of the brainstem to the higher, more complex emotional and cognitive cortical areas. The brain is also born *premature*, with each of the key regions of the brain organising at different times during early childhood in response to a child's early experiences (Perry, 2009). The presence or absence of neuronal stimulation during *sensitive* and *critical periods* of development results in changes to the wiring of the brain (Cozolino, 2002). Hence, the brain is most *plastic* in early childhood and is principally shaped by the quality of a child's earliest relationships. This suggests that developmental trauma has the capacity to cause significantly more disruption than trauma experienced later in life (Perry, 2006). The *use-dependent* nature of the brain also implies that the more frequently a neural pathway is activated the stronger it will become. When a child consistently receives predictable, attuned and nurturing care they develop a neurobiology that enables them to grow into a healthy and resilient adult (Perry, 2006). Alternatively, when a child is consistently exposed to fearful situations they develop a neurobiology that is vulnerable to stress, resulting in difficulties with emotional regulation, relationships, cognition and an increased susceptibility to a range of diseases of the body and mind (Cozolino, 2010; Perry, 2006, 2009; Scaer, 2014).

Fight, flight or freeze

At its core, trauma is a physiological response. In essence, an event is traumatic because of its effect on the nervous system – rather than the nature of the event itself (Levine and Kline, 2007). Scaer (2014) proposes that an experience constitutes trauma when three criteria are present: when there is a perception that one's life is threatened, a sense of helplessness and activation of the fight, flight or freeze response. In many ways trauma is a universal experience, and the fight, flight and freeze response is a natural physiological process that aids survival in situations perceived as threatening. Problems arise when this response is overwhelmed or overused. Levine (1997) believes that disorders of stress and trauma result from an unresolved trauma response, where the trauma cycle has been unable to run to its natural completion, in particular where there has been no opportunity for the nervous system to discharge the *survival energy* harnessed at the time of the original trauma. This energy is then stored in the nervous system, making the individual more vulnerable to future stress. Historically trauma was determined by the nature and severity of the traumatic event, and treatment often involved helping individuals develop a cognitive and language-based understanding of this experience. If trauma is now more broadly understood to be primarily a non-verbal, unresolved physiological response to an event that is perceived as traumatic, intervention is far less about gaining a cognitive understanding of the event and more about working with the unresolved impact of trauma on the body and mind.

This view of trauma has implications for how we understand and treat childhood trauma. If trauma is conceptualised as existing along a continuum that is specific to each individual, this continuum may include experiences that are not commonly considered life threatening but are perceived as life threatening by this person within the context of her previous life experiences (Scaer, 2005). For children, experiences of trauma may begin in the womb. *Pre-verbal trauma* may result from an exposure to high levels of maternal stress hormones, drugs, alcohol or other toxic substances while in utero. A traumatic birth, medical interventions and separation from the caregiver in the hours and days following birth can also constitute trauma for a new infant (Scaer, 2005). Infants by nature are helpless and dependent on their caregivers. If the care that an infant receives is inconsistent, neglectful or abusive, this unfortunately often meets the criteria for trauma. The quality of care that a child receives from her primary caregiver shapes her brain and even influences the expression of her genome. Early pre-verbal experiences of trauma before birth and in the initial years of life set the stage for resilience or vulnerability in the face of future life stress (Scaer, 2005). A serious consequence of early childhood trauma is the disruption caused to a child's developing stress physiology. Many of the behavioural difficulties observed in traumatised children may be the manifestation of unsuccessful attempts to discharge the survival energy they mobilised to defend themselves against threat, which now remains trapped within their bodies (Levine, 1997). These children live with a heightened arousal and reactivity that permeates all they do.

The fear networks in the brain have a fast and a slow system. The fast system originates in the lower brain and communicates with the *amygdala*, the alarm system of the brain. This system is instinctual and makes reflexive, unconscious decisions for immediate survival (Cozolino, 2010). In threatening situations information from the senses immediately activates this alarm, resulting in a fight, flight or freeze response. Typically, a fight or flight response is the first to activate, although in circumstances where death is perceived as imminent or where the fight or flight response is not possible there is a shift to an immobility or freeze state. For infants who are too small to fight or flee, the freeze response is often the only defence available. While the freeze state aids survival in extreme circumstances, there is a growing consensus that it is the lasting effects of an undischarged freeze response that is culpable in the development of disorders of traumatic stress, especially post-traumatic stress disorder (PTSD) (Levine, 1997). In the same way that trauma exists along a continuum, there is growing acknowledgement of the existence of an array of trauma-related disorders in addition to PTSD. Scaer (2005) identifies a spectrum of conditions and trauma symptoms that are related to the fight/flight response (disorders of stress) or the freeze response (disorders of helplessness and dissociation). Within the field of child trauma a number of clinicians support the establishment of a *developmental trauma disorder* as a new framework for encapsulating the symptoms and experiences of children who have histories of complex interpersonal trauma (van der Kolk, 2005).

Hyper-arousal and dissociation

Fight, flight or freeze behaviours can be conceptualised as operating across a hyper-arousal or dissociation continuum (Perry et al., 1995). An individual who is not traumatised tends to remain within the mid-section of either spectrum in a state of inner homeostasis and is able to modulate between states of mild hyper-arousal and dissociation in response to daily stress. When a child is raised in an environment where they are under constant threat, the repeated activation of the fear response may result in the stress response becoming so sensitised that the child remains in a state of constant alarm (Perry, 2006). A child with a sensitised alarm response has a heightened physiological reactivity that makes it difficult for her to maintain a sense of inner homeostasis (van der Kolk, 2005). In the face of an apparently innocuous threat these children rapidly feel intense fear or shame and move into hyper-aroused fight, flight or dissociative freeze states.

Hyper-arousal is linked to the fight/flight response and is a heightened internal sense of arousal that indicates that the nervous system is getting ready to protect against a potential threat that may be internal, external, real or imagined (Levine, 1997). This state of hyper-arousal is accompanied by hyper-vigilance or a sense of being on guard. The feeling of fear is the primary emotion linked to threat and the fight/flight response (Scaer, 2005). Within the playroom a child with a sensitised hyper-arousal system is tuned up and may display traits such as hyper-activity, impulsivity and hyper-vigilance (Perry et al., 1995). An example of hyper-vigilance is the fearful child who routinely startles in response to noises outside the therapy room.

Children in the playroom may re-enact motor elements of the fight/flight response, playing out actions of defence including protective behaviours, such as holding their hands over a body part, or by assuming postures taken at the time of the original trauma (Norton, Ferriegel and Norton, 2011). For example, a child may unconsciously hold a hand over her bottom while beating a toy in a re-enactment of her own experience of physical abuse and her attempts to protect herself at this time (Norton, Ferriegel and Norton, 2011). Children may also play out defensive behaviours through games that involved being chased or chasing, games of hide and seek and pretend attacks or battles that play a role in completing the physical acts of the fight/flight defence that may have been activated but truncated at the time of the original trauma. For children who have become stuck in their defences, play therapy can facilitate the discharge of this stuck survival energy and aid in the completion of the trauma cycle (Norton, Ferriegel and Norton, 2011).

The experience of dissociation is at the other end of the arousal continuum and is linked to the freeze and immobility response. The feeling of shame is associated with this response (Scaer, 2005). Dissociation is a distortion of time and perception. Some experiences of dissociation are universal, such as daydreaming, although more extreme forms of dissociation involve a sense of disconnect to the point that an individual is no longer orientated to where they are in time or space. A child with a sensitised dissociative system may display avoidant, depressed, defiant or dissociative behaviours (Perry et al., 1995). These children appear cut off from their internal world and are often unaware of their own physical discomfort; for example, they will continue to wear a jumper when they are obviously hot, seem unaware of feeling thirsty, not respond to pain when they accidentally injure themselves or assume and maintain uncomfortable positions for play. These children may also appear clumsy, walking over toys and bumping into walls or furniture. They may forget where they have placed items during their play and also struggle to visually scan for and find particular toys when needed.

There is an evident link between childhood trauma and sensory processing difficulties with children presenting as either over- or under-responsive to sensory input or fluctuating between the two extremes. Children with a sensitised dissociative system appear to be under-responsive to both their internal and external sensory worlds. This makes sense given that the freeze response is designed to help an individual cut off from unbearable sensations and emotions. These children may also be observed to assume frozen postures, tune out and stare into space, often following intense sequences of play. Other types of avoidant and dissociative behaviours might include ending sessions early, taking multiple toilet breaks, abrupt changes in play, refusing to attend therapy following a difficult session or, like Jay, avoiding a certain type of play or toys, such as the dollhouse, for some sessions. Play themes related to death, escape and disappearing might also be a symbolic expression of the experience of dissociation for these children (Norton, Ferriegel and Norton, 2011).

Memory and survival

Our perception of danger largely comes from sensations within our bodies that are implicitly related to threat. Our memory systems are especially sensitive to storing memories that are important to survival. If the fast system of the fear response is activated due to threat, the lower areas of the brain and the nervous system store the pattern of sensory input linked to this threat as an *implicit* or *state memory*, so that the alarm response can immediately activate the next time this same pattern of sensory input is detected (Perry, 2006). Implicit memories are unconscious, procedural memories and encapsulate the things we do without thinking. They are different from *explicit memories*, which are conscious, declarative memories. Explicit memories are more closely linked to the slow system of the fear response, which reviews threatening experiences and gives conscious meaning to the physical and emotional responses already enacted by the fast system (Cozolino, 2010).

Therapists need to be sensitive to a child's implicit memory system and the *kindled* state of the brain's alarm response (Scaer, 2005). Within therapy it is likely that a child will experience unconscious internal or external reminders of their own traumatic experiences at an implicit level that may activate their alarm system and cause them to move into hyper-aroused or dissociative states. An obvious example is the child who flinches when you move or stand too quickly, the child appearing to anticipate an act of aggression. Implicit reminders of trauma may be more subtle and stem from something within the child's play, something in the playroom, or something about the therapist, be it her appearance, the way she moves, her mannerisms, how she sounds or even smells, that is implicitly related to threat for this child. In many ways post-traumatic play is driven by this unconscious, implicit world of stored trauma memories, which is why post-traumatic play needs to be handled with care so that it does not re-traumatise the child and further entrench these fear-based trauma memories.

When implicit memories surface within therapy, the goal is to *reconsolidate* rather than relive these memories so that they are reintegrated in a less troubling form (Panksepp and Biven, 2012). Reconsolidation is achieved when a traumatic memory is linked to a new, more positive affective experience. This may be achieved purely through the child accessing this memory while she is engaged in play with a safe and supportive adult, given that play is an intrinsically rewarding process in the brain (Panksepp and Biven, 2012). Play is a means by which these memories can be revised and newly associated with a positive affective experience, which may assist in removing the string from these memories so they no longer trigger a fear response.

Post-traumatic play

Children are naturally compelled to play out troubling and traumatic experiences. This innate tendency for children to express their feelings and experiences through play is the foundation of play therapy, although Jay's play illustrates that not all play is intrinsically therapeutic. When working with children and trauma, therapists must distinguish between traumatic play, traumatic re-enactment and the re-working of trauma (Levine, 1997). The type of play displayed by Jay does not aid in the re-working of trauma and has been labelled *stuck play* (Goodyear-Brown, 2010) or *stagnant post-traumatic play* (Gil, 2006). In stuck play children tend to be unaware of the presence of the therapist. This play also lacks imagination, joy, spontaneity and variety and fails to bring relief (Gil, 2006; Levine and Kline, 2007). Alternatively, *dynamic post-traumatic play* allows for the re-working of trauma and is characterised by visible affect, variety, creativity, imagination, symbolism, joy and relief and an acknowledgement of and interaction with the therapist (Gil, 2006). In essence, it could be argued that stuck play is not really play at all, as it is missing the defining element of play, largely joy in relationship. Panksepp identifies play as one of the seven basic affective and motivational systems for the mammalian brain (Panksepp and Biven, 2012). He asserts that play has its own unique neural circuitry that can only be accessed when a child is feeling safe. Stuck play appears to be removed from this play circuitry and indicates that a child is not reintegrating her trauma but potentially re-experiencing it. Theoretically, dynamic play occurs when three elements are present: an active play circuitry, a perception of safety and a supportive relationship.

Dynamic play is the type of play therapists hope to facilitate. When a child is engaged in dynamic play we can be confident that a child's play circuitry is activated and her attachment system is online, enabling her to utilise both play and the therapeutic relationship to attain an optimal state of physiological and psychological arousal that best facilitates the reworking and integration of trauma, without triggering defensive fight, flight or freeze reactions. There also seems to be something unique to the play circuitry of the brain that means that play, by its very nature, allows for higher levels of arousal without activation of the fear response. Panksepp advocates that play should have a greater role within the field of psychotherapy given that play actually changes the brain, promotes neural integration, aids in the creation of social circuits and is an "inestimable boon" to a child's "self-esteem and feelings of friendliness to others" (Panksepp and Biven, 2012: 385).

Once a child is in a position where they are able to tolerate a degree of stress within therapy, therapy can then move to address higher emotional and cognitive issues such as trauma narratives, meaning, guilt, shame, loss and identity (Heller and LaPierre, 2012; Steele and Malchiodi, 2012). Through play, children can gain a symbolic mastery over their fear that can effect real change in their neurobiology (Norton, Ferriegel and Norton, 2011). Symbolic expression through art, movement and play provides a means through which children can complete previously truncated acts of defence, which changes the meaning of these experiences and leads to feelings of mastery, pride and empowerment (Scaer, 2005; Norton, Ferriegel and Norton, 2011). The feeling of helplessness is one of the most disabling elements of trauma. The opportunity to overcome this feeling and replace it with a sense of mastery and control, even symbolically, is one of the keys to healing from trauma (Scaer, 2005). Through symbolic play children can experiment with alternative endings and build a sense of safety and mastery. As Goodyear-Brown notes (2010: 65):

> Through the many repetitions of safe outcomes that are experienced through metaphoric play, the client begins to build an alternative script to the one of danger that has previously been rehearsed. In the same way that sensations of helplessness and terror can be conditioned through traumatic experiences, sensations of empowerment and security can be conditioned through repetitions of energized, experiential play.

A key marker that distinguishes dynamic therapeutic play from stuck play is the experience of joy. Carroll (2002) in her study of children's play therapy experiences found that having fun was one of the things children most valued about therapy. Play is a primary source of motivation and joy (Panksepp and Biven, 2012). If a child's play is joyless, a therapist should question the state of the child's nervous system, as it is likely that the child is no longer playing within her *window of tolerance*. Equally, we must remember that for a traumatised child the experience of joy itself might be so foreign that it is also a source of stress (Warner, Cook, Westcott and Koomar, 2011). Part of widening a child's window of tolerance is to help her nervous system tolerate not only intense emotions linked to fear and shame but also those linked to joy and excitement without becoming overwhelmed. Levine (1997) observes that one of the key symptoms of trauma is a diminished capacity for curiosity and joy. When curiosity and joy are observed within therapy this is a sign that the child is developing a greater sense of safety and beginning to integrate her traumatic experiences. Ultimately, when a child is dynamically re-working her trauma there is a sense of relief, release, joy and achievement as she gains mastery over the intense and scary feelings associated with past traumas. Moments of shared joy within therapy are of great therapeutic value, and therapists should aim to consolidate these "rare but precious moments where pain can be turned into joy" (Panksepp and Biven, 2012: 435).

The window of tolerance

When children play out traumatic experiences they will inevitably evoke emotional and physiological memories associated with the original trauma. However, if a child is to integrate traumatic experiences they must have a controlled exposure to these implicit memories. Either extreme of the physiological arousal spectrum, states of hyper-arousal or dissociation, hinders the integration of traumatic experiences. Practitioners refer to a desired physiological arousal window or *window of tolerance* that best facilitates the safe processing of traumatic material (Ogden, Minton and Pain, 2006) and, by inference, dynamic play. Stagnant or stuck play results when a child is outside the bounds of her therapeutic window and is no longer in a safe physiological state. It is widely acknowledged that some stress is necessary to create change in therapy. The challenge for the therapists is to keep a child within the window where there is an optimal level of nervous system activation in which the re-working of trauma and neural integration can best take place, so that they are neither disconnected nor overwhelmed by their experience of therapy (Cozolino, 2010). The renegotiation of trauma must occur in a titrated fashion, so that the level of arousal increases at a similar rate as the development of a child's internal resources for managing stress (Levine, 1997).

A key role of the play therapist is as an *affect regulator*, who assists in soothing the physiology of a child (Goodyear-Brown, 2010). A play therapist should have an acute understanding of a child's position on the arousal continuum and carefully attune to the physiological state of a child through observing physical markers, such as body position and movement, tension, respiration, facial expression and changes in skin colour. These markers help a therapist determine how a child's nervous system is managing the stress that comes with re-working trauma (Heller and LaPierre, 2012). These observations direct the therapist in knowing when to talk and when to use simple nonverbal communication, when to experiment with changes in pace, tone and volume of voice and when to change her posture and distance from the child in order to keep the child within her window of tolerance so that she is not overwhelmed by her experience of therapy (Ogden, Minton and Pain, 2006; Perry, 2006). If the fear response is activated, a therapist must then act in a way that assists the child to regain a sense of safety and move back into her window of tolerance (Warner, Cook, Westcott and Koomar, 2011). Through tracking a child's bodily states a therapist can help ground a child in the present and keep her from becoming overwhelmed or disconnected while playing about her past. From this safe psychological and safe physiological state a child can re-examine her "traumas without repeating them and making them real once again" (van der Kolk, 2005: 408).

Levine (1997) outlines a number of principles for working with children and trauma that are relevant to play therapy and a useful guide in how to keep a child within her window of tolerance.

1   *Let the child control the pace of the game.* One of the strengths of child-led play therapy is that it allows children to experience a sense of control over the pace of trauma work.
2   *Distinguish among fear, terror and excitement.* Within a child's play, fear and terror are associated with a state of helplessness; excitement and joy, on the other hand, indicate that a child is successfully discharging some of the powerful emotions linked to trauma. An aim of therapy is to make unbearable feelings bearable by adding new affective experiences to these traumatic memories, which is often evidenced by the presence of joyful, dynamic play.
3   *Take one small step at a time.* Re-working traumatic experiences takes time. There is a rhythm to trauma work in which the child moves toward and away from trauma content several times over as part of the reparative process. One of the key differences between stuck and dynamic post-traumatic play is that

dynamic play includes incremental differences in the child's play. Levine (1997) notes that it does not matter how many times a child might repeat a sequence of play; if the child shows subtle changes in how she responds, with changes in her voice, level of excitement, amount of speech or spontaneous movements, this indicates that a child is moving through her trauma.

4   *Be patient – a good container.* A therapist must believe that a child is capable of re-working her traumatic experiences, which in turn gives the child confidence and hope.

5   *If you feel that the child is genuinely not benefiting from the play, stop.* If a therapist observes that a child is becoming overwhelmed by her play she has a responsibility to intervene and help shift the child back into her window of tolerance. Often a play therapist's use of tracking and reflecting is sufficient to achieve this. If this is unsuccessful a therapist may need to take a more directive approach to shift this play through suggesting subtle changes in play, position or movement for the child.

Engaging the lower brain

The parts of the brain that are developing during a period of trauma are the parts of the brain that will be most disrupted. By reason, any intervention must therefore target these areas of the brain (Perry, 2009). Children who have experienced trauma in the first years of life, while the lower stress regulatory parts of the brain are developing, may present with extremely narrow windows of tolerance. For these children therapeutic intervention must initially focus on building a more resilient nervous system and widening this physiological window so that they are better equipped to manage the stress that comes with trauma work (Levine and Kline, 2007). Play therapy must engage the lower brain and intervene at a pre-symbolic sensorimotor level before moving to metaphoric play. The lower stress response networks in the brain cannot be accessed via language and can only be reorganised through patterned and repetitive sensory and body-based interventions (Gaskell, 2008; Perry, 2009). This means that the sensory and motor elements of play are vital for these children, especially in the early stages of therapy.

In part, play and the play materials themselves provide sensory experiences that help regulate a child's stress physiology. Play, by nature, is a multisensory experience, and "it is impossible for children to play without moving their bodies" (Panksepp and Biven, 2012: 464). Commonly used sensory- and motor-based play materials, such as musical instruments, paint, dough, clay, sand and water, can be used by a child to calm her nervous system. Play involves many senses at any one time and encompasses the visual, tactile, auditory, vestibular, kinaesthetic and proprioceptive senses. The proprioceptive sense is of particular interest as it can have a powerfully soothing and regulatory impact on the nervous system. The proprioceptive system provides feedback via muscles and joints as to our body's position in space (Warner, Cook, Westcott and Koomar, 2011). Play and materials that provide deep resistance through pushing, pulling, lifting, throwing, drumming, crashing and squeezing activate this system and sooth the nervous system. The sensory experience of play has a unique ability to "pull the brain together" and encourages *vertical integration*, especially in the right hemisphere; forming links between the body (sensations), lower brain (instincts), limbic brain (emotions) and the cortex (cognition; Badenoch, 2008).

In light of the need to engage the lower brain in trauma work, play therapists need to think about how they might capitalise on the body- and sensory-based experiences that are available in therapy. Where possible a playroom should be a sensory-enriched environment that provides a number of possible outlets for sensory and motor play. There is room within the practice of play therapy to consider incorporating a wider array of sensory experiences that aid in integration of the lower brain. Equipment such as weighted toys or blankets, posture balls, the use of Lycra, body socks and other pieces of equipment that allow for swathing, rocking and swinging could also be incorporated into the playroom. This equipment would allow for sensory experiences that replicate early attachment experiences, such as the feeling of being held and rocked, that are crucial in building the lower brain and regulatory stress networks. The provision of a greater array of sensorimotor experiences that replicate early sensory experiences within the attachment relationship may prove reparative for children who have missed out on these foundational experiences. It must also be acknowledged that early trauma can be so disruptive to brain development that a child will need of an array of therapeutic supports in addition to play therapy to truly aid in healing the lower parts of the brain. Perry (2006) advocates for a *neurosequential* approach in which interventions are matched to a child's specific developmental and physiological needs within the context of a relationally enriched *therapeutic web*.

The therapeutic relationship

Recent advances in neuroscience support the centrality of the therapeutic relationship in treatment outcome (Steele and Malchiodi, 2012). In fact, supportive relationships may be the most crucial element in healing from trauma (Scaer, 2005). Cozolino (2010) postulates that Carl Rogers's (1980) core conditions (empathy, unconditional positive regard and congruence) describe the ideal interpersonal relationship for changing the brain, creating an optimal physiological environment for neural integration. It is widely agreed that the capacity of the therapist for attunement and genuine empathy is at the heart of treatment success. In many ways the therapeutic relationship mirrors the neurobiology of the early attachment relationship (Steele and Malchiodi, 2012). A secure, attuned therapeutic relationship serves to inhibit the fear networks in the brain and encodes new implicit memories of a positive and caring relationship (Cozolino, 2010). Where sensory play aids in the vertical integration of the brain, the right-to-right hemisphere connection between the right brain of the therapist and the right brain of the child aids in *horizontal integration*, helping to rewire the brain in the direction of secure patterns of attachment (Badenoch, 2008). In the same way that the quality of the early attachment relationship shapes the brain, for better or worse, the quality of the therapeutic relationship determines the degree to which therapy changes the brain.

Porges (2011), in his *polyvagal theory*, focuses on the process through which the *social engagement system*, including attachment relationships, can inhibit defence mechanisms and delineates between a *neuroception* of danger, safety or life threat. Neuroception refers to the unconscious, continuous risk assessment of our internal and external environment. The polyvagal theory proposes that there are two branches of the *vagus* cranial nerve that regulate behaviour. One branch, the *ventral vagus*, inhibits the fight/flight response and facilitates social interactions in environments that are perceived as safe. This branch of the vagus is also involved in key attachment behaviours including the perception of facial expressions, tone of voice and attuned listening. The second branch, the *dorsal vagus*, facilitates defensive reactions in the face of danger, with separate neural circuits for mobilisation (fight, flight) and immobilisation (freeze). When there is a neuroception of safety, the vagus nerve and the social engagement system actively inhibit the lower brain areas that control fight, flight or freeze behaviours. Alternatively, when there is a neuroception of danger, the social engagement system is inhibited and defence systems activated (Porges, 2011).

Developmental trauma is problematic, as it can reset the autonomic nervous system so that it develops a bias towards defensive reactions rather than social engagement. Thus, the nervous system of a traumatised child may display a distorted neuroception and an inclination for defensive fight or flight behaviours, even in the absence of threat. In states of mobilisation the social engagement system shuts down, making it difficult for these children to engage and feel safe with others. This theory highlights the importance of the therapeutic relationship, especially when working with the fear networks in the brain. The therapeutic relationship, via the vagus nerve, plays a central role in containing fear and defensive fight, flight or freeze reactions. The play therapist's presence actually contributes to changes in the very parts of the brain that manage pain, fear, anxiety and distress (Scaer, 2005).

Return to the dollhouse

For Jay, frightening experiences within the home and her early attachment relationships likely resulted in repeated activation of her fight, flight or freeze response. It could be hypothesised that Jay's initial play sequence was evidence of a vulnerable and sensitised physiology resulting from known and unknown experiences of early trauma. Her neuroception was distorted, causing her to sense danger rather than safety in her initial play therapy session. With her defence systems activated she became stuck in a cycle of repetitive post-traumatic play. In the early stages of therapy a child is at a greater risk of becoming overwhelmed by her play, as there has not been sufficient time to establish a sense of psychological and physiological safety within the context of a secure therapeutic relationship. This is a time when therapists need to be particularly sensitive to children, like Jay, who have not had the early experiences necessary to help them learn how to effectively regulate stress. These children are most at risk of being caught off guard and unexpectedly stumbling into stagnant post-traumatic play sequences.

As therapy progressed I attempted to attune better to Jay's psychological and physiological states. For a number of sessions Jay chose to engage primarily in sensory play with sand, water and paint. Intuitively she seemed to be seeking out sensory activities that regulated the lower parts of her brain and soothed her sensitised fear networks. Eventually a sense of safety was restored and Jay returned to the dollhouse. A number of changes were now evident in Jay's play; while themes of violence and fear persisted along with the same banging, hiding and discovery of dolls, Jay's play was more varied, fluid and animated, and she showed relief and joy within her play. She now displayed emotion on behalf of the dolls, taking sharp breaths to indicate fear and surprise. Jay also discovered a way to regulate her arousal, frequently alternating between play in the dollhouse and sucking water from a baby's bottle.

Porges (2011) pays special attention to the role of nursing/sucking in creating calm behavioural and visceral states and dampening defensive reactions via the vagus nerve, linking early nursing behaviours to the development of social engagement behaviours. Similarly, Jay was using the baby's bottle as a way to self-regulate and titrate her exposure to the stress of playing about her early trauma. Jay's play took on a rhythmic quality as she danced to and from the dollhouse and the baby's bottle. As Jay's window of tolerance grew larger, she gradually tolerated longer and longer periods of play in the dollhouse, with a growing sense of mastery and control. New dolls were introduced that served the role of a protector or rescuer. These dolls took the baby dolls from the house and retaliated and defended the child dolls against the aggressors. Towards the end of her therapy Jay's dollhouse play began to reflect her current foster home. Through her play Jay appeared to be building a bridge between her past and present experiences and was no longer overwhelmed by memories of her traumatic past. Her play had moved from being stuck to dynamic.

For therapists who work with childhood trauma, defensive behaviours linked to the fear response inevitably present in therapy to varying degrees, especially states of hyper-arousal and dissociation, although it is preferable to prevent children from re-experiencing their trauma through triggering a full-blown fight, flight or freeze response. The challenge for play therapists working with early trauma is to simultaneously widen each child's unique window of tolerance for stress whilst keeping the child within this changing and ideally expanding window. For some children the degree of early trauma experienced may result in a fragile nervous system and a narrow window of tolerance. In these instances the therapist must first work with the lower stress-regulatory parts of the brain, capitalising on the sensory and body based mechanisms that are intrinsic to play therapy. The activation of the social engagement system through the therapeutic relationship also plays a vital role in dampening the neural circuits that control fight, flight and freeze reactions. Therapeutic, dynamic play occurs when a child remains within her window of tolerance and feels safe and connected to another person. Dynamic play provides a means through which children can tame intense emotions, especially those related to stress, shame and fear, and internalise and reconsolidate new implicit memories of a safe, positive and enjoyable relationship.

The effectiveness of play therapy has long been witnessed by practicing play therapists and now has a growing basis of support arising from within the field of neuroscience. Play therapy is unique in that it can draw on the neurobiological mechanism of play and relationship, which are two powerful means for regulating arousal and taming the fear response. Play and the therapeutic relationship create an ideal neurobiological environment for neural integration and growth and can actually change the brain in a positive way. Through play, trauma memories can be re-worked at both a metaphorical and a neurobiological level. Timely play therapy intervention for children who have experienced early trauma may prove salient in the prevention of future stress and trauma-related illnesses of the body and mind. Finally, play therapy is also unique, in that play is an intrinsically rewarding experience. The experience of joy within the therapeutic relationship further aids healing from trauma, with "therapeutic moments of mutually shared joy" being perhaps, "one of the greater emotional gifts that psychotherapy can ever provide" (Panksepp and Biven, 2012: 467).

Note

1 Jay is a pseudonym. Her story is based on composite material from clinical experience, and details have been changed to protect confidentiality. The female pronoun will be used throughout to simplify the text and further illustrate this case study.

References

Badenoch, B. (2008) *Being a Brain-Wise Therapist: A Practical Guide to Interpersonal Neurobiology*. New York: W. W. Norton & Company.

Carroll, J. (2002) Play Therapy: The Children's Views. *Child and Family Social Work* Vol 7, 177–187.

Cozolino, L. (2002) *The Neuroscience of Psychotherapy: Building and Rebuilding the Human Brain*. New York: W. W. Norton & Company.

Cozolino, L. (2010) *The Neuroscience of Psychotherapy: Healing the Social Brain*, 2nd Edn. New York: W. W. Norton & Company.

Gaskell, R. (2008) *Neuroscience and Play Therapy*. California: Association for Play Therapy Mining.

Gil, E. (2006) *Helping Abused and Traumatised Children: Integrating Directive and Non-directive Approaches*. New York: Guildford Press.

Goodyear-Brown, P. (2010) *Play Therapy with Traumatised Children: A Prescriptive Approach*. Hoboken, NJ: John Wiley & Sons, Inc.

Heller, L. & LaPierre, A. (2012) *Healing Developmental Trauma*. Berkeley, CA: North Atlantic Books.

Levine, P.A. (1997) *Walking the Tiger Healing Trauma*. Berkeley, CA: North Atlantic Books.

Levine, P.A. & Kline, M. (2007) *Trauma Through a Child's Eyes*. Berkeley, CA: North Atlantic Books.

Norton, B., Ferriegel, M. & Norton, C. (2011) Somatic Expressions of Trauma in Experiential Play. *International Journal of Play Therapy* Vol 20 (3), 138–152.

Ogden, P., Minton, K. & Pain, C. (2006) *Trauma and the Body: A Sensorimotor Approach to Psychotherapy*. New York: W.W. Norton & Company.

Panksepp, J. & Biven, L. (2012) *The Archaeology of the Mind: Neuroevolutionary Origins of Human Emotions*. New York: W.W. Norton & Company.

Perry, B. (2006) Applying Principles of Neurodevelopment to Clinical Work with Maltreated and Traumatized Children. In: Webb, N.B. (ed) *Working with Traumatized Children in Child Welfare* (pp. 27–52). New York: Guilford Press.

Perry, B. (2009) Examining Child Maltreatment through a Neurodevelopmental Lens: Clinical Applications of the Neurosequential Model of Therapeutics. *Journal of Loss and Trauma* Vol 14, 240–255.

Perry, B., Pollard, R.A., Blakley, T.L., Baker, W.L. & Vigilante, D. (1995) Childhood Trauma, the Neurobiology of Adaptation, and "Use-dependent" Development of the Brain: How "States" Becomes "Traits." *Infant Mental Health Journal* Vol 16 (4), 271–291.

Porges, S.W. (2011) *The Polyvagal Theory: Neurophysiological Foundations of Emotions, Attachment, Communication, Self-regulation*. New York: W.W. Norton & Company.

Rogers, C.R. (1980) *A Way of Being*. Boston: Houghton Mifflin.

Rothschild, B. (2000) *The Body Remembers: The Psychophysiology of Trauma and Trauma Treatment*. New York: W.W. Norton & Company.

Scaer, R. (2005) *The Trauma Spectrum: Hidden Wounds and Human Resiliency*. New York: W.W. Norton & Company.

Scaer, R. (2014) *The Body Bears the Burden: Trauma, Dissociation and Disease*, 3rd Edn. New York: Routledge.

Steele, W. & Malchiodi, C.A. (2012) *Trauma-Informed Practices with Children and Adolescents*. New York: Routledge.

Van der Kolk, B. (2005) Developmental Trauma Disorder: Towards a Rational Diagnosis for Children with Complex Trauma Histories. *Psychiatric Annals* Vol 35 (5), 401–108.

Warner, E., Cook, A., Westcott, A. & Koomar, J. (2011) *SMART Sensory Motor Arousal Regulation Treatment: A Manual for Therapists Working with Children and Adolescents. A "Bottom-Up" Approach to Treatment and Complex Trauma*. Brookline, MA: The Trauma Centre at JRI.

Chapter 6

Who am I now?

How play therapy can empower children and adolescents in their 'search for self' following severe acquired brain injury

Jan Vance

Ariadne's thread

Ancient myths and legends have a power to inspire, sustain and nurture us. The myth of Ariadne and the thread she gave to Theseus, so that he would be able to find his way back through the labyrinth after he had slain the Minotaur, is one such myth, and her thread is a powerful metaphor to describe the power of the therapeutic relationship. Imagine if you will a labyrinth containing the 'beast' of severe acquired brain injury. Imagine last remembering going out for a walk to the shops but now finding yourself in a world of terrifyingly strange noises and lights, unable to move, speak, eat or make any sense of who you are. Or imagine being told you are going into hospital for a routine operation to remove a swelling in your head causing you to have headaches and feel sick, but you awake paralysed. You are told your brain has been hurt, but what is a brain and who am I now if I have an injured brain? Although a child's full sense of self is not developed until their late teens (Harter, 1999), and brain injury can result in a lack of insight about the injury (Catroppa et al., 2012; Cicerone et al., 2000), children and adolescents with brain injury still suffer a distressing dislocation of their sense of self.

Such was my world for nine years, during which time I supported more than 90 children and adolescents as a lone play therapy practitioner within a medically-driven residential rehabilitation unit for paediatric severe acquired brain injury. The children and adolescents arrived at the unit in what is known, medically, as a 'sub-acute phase' following their discharge from an acute hospital. In this sub-acute phase, there is still potential for on-going recovery of function and skills, but the recovery journey is uncertain, and the language of medical and therapy staff is not one of cure but of optimizing potential.

Recent years have seen increasing interest, albeit with reference primarily to the adult brain-injured population, in the concept of a 'loss of self' and its painful grief and longing for 'life to be as it was' (Lennon et al., 2014) and how "the re-development of identity seems a particularly important, but often neglected focus for rehabilitation" (Muenchberger, Kendall and Neal, 2008: 980). The concept of post-trauma growth goes further, postulating that positive psychological changes can be achieved following trauma or adversity, such as greater appreciation of life and discovery of unexpected personal strengths, and this concept is being increasingly used to guide the counselling of adults with brain injury (Collicutt McGrath, 2011). My hypothesis was that with play therapy support, brain-injured children and adolescents might also experience 'green shoots' of post-trauma growth breaking through the heavy 'soil' of their emotional distress. But I move too fast.

First, I must take you on my own journey, learning how 'to spin a thread' strong enough to withstand the rigours of journeying through the labyrinth of severe acquired brain injury. How I discovered how loosely or tightly I needed to let the thread out and how at times keeping hold of it challenged not only my own professional development and confidence but also threatened to overwhelm me with a desire to 'let it go'. An experience of compassion fatigue which risked becoming a secondary trauma response, a risk all play therapists face when confronted with immense emotional pain and distress (Figley, 1995).

So what I wish to share with you is how I adapted and developed my own play therapy practice to support this traumatised client group. How invaluable good teamwork was to this process and what a crucial role my own play therapy supervision played in enabling me to 'keep hold of that thread'.

The labyrinth on an 'island of dreams'

Dreams can be good or bad. They can be terrifying or joyous, confusing or clarifying, full of despair or full of hope. The residential rehabilitation unit, an island far from home on which the children and their families found themselves marooned and where the Minotaur 'beast' of severe brain injury lived in his labyrinth was indeed an island of dreams, good and bad. Each child had a unique constellation of impairments dependent on the specific nature of their brain injury. So the rehabilitation unit had many continuums, for example, from those in a minimally conscious state through to those fully conscious or from those with independent mobility to those paralysed. It could be a deeply shocking place of distressing sights and sounds, and the children evidenced wide variance in physical, cognitive, behavioural and emotional functioning and in their pre-injury life experience.

"I have landed on an island of kindness – no sharks here – just rainbow-coloured fish", was what one eight-year-old boy said to me shortly after we had first met. He had spent five months in an acute hospital, recovering from a stroke he had tragically sustained during a surgical procedure, a stroke that had left him consciously aware but for some weeks unable to move or speak. He had made a remarkable recovery regarding cognition, mobility and speech, but his swallow and coughing reflexes were still badly affected, leaving him reliant on a tracheostomy and unable to eat. Although greatly distressed about this, he was able to orientate himself accurately in a rehabilitation setting and was full of hope. But for another 10-year-old girl, who had suddenly collapsed from a devastating brain haemorrhage four months previously and was still experiencing balance and memory impairments, arriving at the 'island' was a bewildering experience. She was very scared. "Tell me this is all a bad dream and that I am going to wake up soon", she begged me in her first play therapy session. Another child arriving at the unit and still disorientated from his brain tumour removal said, "Aliens must have captured me and taken me to another planet".

Indeed, sometimes this 'island', so remote from anything the parents could have imagined would ever be the destination for their healthy, normal child, was equally nightmarish to them. They often felt shocked when confronted with the reality of the rehabilitation unit, a setting that could be even more distressing to them than the acute hospital, where a range of illnesses and the possibility of cure and complete recovery existed. Here all the children had brain injury, and life for all of them would never be the same as before (Catroppa et al., 2012).

For children living on the unit and for their family members staying on site, this was, however, a temporary home with therapy programmes typically lasting between 12 and 36 weeks. There were of course many others on 'the island' too: doctors, nurses, therapists, social workers, teachers, carers, caterers, cleaners, gardeners and office staff. The philosophy of the unit was that rehabilitation was 24 hour, requiring all staff to gain an understanding of at least the rudiments of brain injury so they could interact in ways that were helpful rather than harmful to a child's recovery (Ylvisaker, 1998).

However, I and other members of the therapy team, physiotherapists, speech and language therapists, occupational therapists, clinical and educational psychologists, needed to know significantly more about brain injury to comprehend the contributions of other members of the multi-disciplinary team. As I had no prior medical knowledge of brain injury, this was an especially exacting challenge.

The 'Minotaur' of severe acquired brain injury

Ariadne did not herself meet the Minotaur. She had no direct experience of its horrors. But she needed to appreciate the beast's shape to comprehend its power to terrify. I needed to do likewise. As a lone play therapy practitioner in a residential, medically driven rehabilitation unit, I crucially had to gain the professional respect of my colleagues if my intervention was to be given opportunity. I would have to show that for children with brain injury, who easily fatigue, time spent with me would assist their rehabilitation and was therefore an appropriate therapy for them to receive within their weekly timetable of sessions. So it was imperative that I showed sufficient understanding of the specific nature of the brain injury each child had sustained.

Respect is of course never a given but has to be continually earned. It springs from colleagues witnessing, not only your dedication and commitment to your specialism and belief in the positive outcomes it achieves but also from your appreciation of theirs. I therefore prioritised my attendance at team meetings and sought out informal colleague contact to discuss how a child was progressing. I studied texts on how the brain works, gaining a deep appreciation of its intricacy. I discovered how much humility there is within present-day neuroscience, with the brain still seen as our 'final frontier', a place of incomprehensible beauty and wonder yet to be unravelled. "The brain still remains a tantalising mystery: to those of us who have been studying it for most of our lives it often seems the more we learn, the more there is still to learn" (Greenfield, 1998: xvi).

An on-going controversy of particular relevance because of its key importance to paediatric brain injury concerned the neuroplasticity and growth potential of the young brain to repair damage versus its greater vulnerability to brain injury because of its immaturity. However, it seemed neither early plasticity nor early vulnerability perspectives were able to explain the full range of outcomes following early brain insult. Each could be seen to represent an oversimplification of the multiple complexities at play. There remained "a need for long term follow up of such children to identify whether the apparent more severe consequences from injury for younger children indicated a permanent deficit or a delayed maturation and slowed recovery process" (Anderson, Catroppa Morse, et al., 2005: 1382). However, much persuasive evidence exists that "[c]hildren are more vulnerable to trauma than adults. [. . .] Experience in adults alters the organised brain, but in infants and children it organises the developing brain" (Perry and Pollard, 1998: 36). I hoped that through their experiencing a therapeutic relationship with me, I could have a positive organising influence on that developing, albeit injured, brain.

I learnt to identify the ways in which our brain is the command centre of our being. How it is the 'puppeteer', pulling all the strings that make our bodies work and telling us who we are. How each and every brain injury is thoroughly unique, be it traumatic, the result of an impact injury to the head such as in a car accident, or atraumatic, such as from a brain tumour, a haemorrhage or a viral infection. How a primarily focal injury damaged a specific area, but a more global injury spread throughout the brain, affecting many functions.

As the rehabilitation unit was residential, it treated the more severe end of the brain injury continuum. So children and adolescents would often be in wheelchairs, having lost control of body movement, and they were likely to have additional impairments involving possibly breathing and eating, receptive and/or expressive language, and cognitive deficits in memory, attention and the executive functioning skills of organisation, planning and sequencing. Even for the children who had achieved physical recovery, regaining their ability to walk, talk and eat, there was often more subtle evidence that they still had upsetting cognitive impairments affecting their executive functioning skills and personalities. They were often referred to by staff as 'the walking wounded'. There might also be organic injury to their emotional regulatory systems, and there was a wide-range of behavioural difficulties caused by a complex combination of organic injury, trauma experiences and the suddenness of their changed capabilities and identities. Moreover, medical interventions were also continuing to blight their present, as they continued to need medical tests and monitoring.

There is however strong evidence for the efficacy of play therapy for children facing medical procedures and for those suffering chronic illness (Jones and

Landreth, 2002) and, more widely, evidence from meta-analyses in support of play therapy for anxiety, withdrawal, emotional lability, learning difficulty, attention deficit hyperactivity and disaster victims (Ray, Schottelkorb and Tsai, 2007; Baggerly and Bratton, 2010). "Play therapy is the recommended therapeutic medium because play . . . enables the child to distance from traumatic events through the use of symbolic materials" (Webb, 2001: 291). All the children invariably seemed changed to their families. Inevitably any serious injury changes a child because it subjects them to so many terrifying ordeals – but this 'change' was also deeper, coming as it did from an inter-play of organic brain injury and psychological trauma. The parents would have to learn to love this 'new child' (Braga et al., 2005).

So the Minotaur took shape for me. I was no expert on it, but I could appreciate its devastating power. Against this Minotaur, however, I had one powerful weapon. I had been inspired by the analogy that as play therapists we are 'brain sculptors' (Sunderland, 2006). If I could trust the child to choose how best to allow their injured brain to experience the therapeutic alliance I was offering, and if they could sense sufficient relationship with me to allow them to explore the twists and turns of their labyrinth narrative, then possibly I could 'sculpt' their brain in ways that would not only support their psychological recovery but also assist organic recovery. I would be working at that frontier of how the brain experiences relationship. Possibly in the decades ahead we will have a much better understanding of how play therapy affects brain functioning, but for us now it is still the 'Dark Ages'. "There are ridiculously simple questions about the cortex that we can't answer at all" (Reid, cited in Zimmer, 2014: 51).

Spinning the thread

How best, I wondered, could I spin a play therapy thread, strong enough yet flexible enough to guide, encourage and sustain deeply injured, troubled and confused children whose identities had been torn cruelly from them by random acts of illness or accident. This thread would need to be talismanic for each child as they journeyed forth to confront their Minotaur, a Minotaur that could metamorphose into bewildering behavioural polarities, shifting from aggression to appeasement, excitability to passivity, perseveration to impulsivity, dis-inhibition to withdrawal.

It would need to be a thread a 3-year-old or a 17-year-old could hold, a mute or garrulous child could 'hear', a blind child could sense, a paralysed or a walking child could use. A thread suited to a child who could not eat or to a child who could not control their eating impulse. A thread for a child with impaired memory, disorientated on the threshold of the labyrinth, or for a child with trauma memories so severe that venturing a foot forward filled them with dread. A thread that could strengthen in eight weeks but also, for another child, last a year. The thread would also need not to threaten other therapists or parents.

My overriding criterion for offering play therapy was, however, that, despite fatigue and impairments, the child needed to possess sufficient cognition to be able to 'know' my thread was there, because ultimately the therapeutic thread is a relationship (Landreth, 2002). It is not the toys, it is not even the child's own play choices, but it is how they are helped to make better sense of those play choices through the trust they develop in their relationship with their therapist that I have always believed is the utterly crucial ingredient. The play therapy mantra that 'the healing is in the relationship' has always been my bedrock. But a thread needs a spool if it is not to be a tangled mess, and it needs to be let out evenly and at a pace to suit 'the one' who pulls it.

The spool

The thread of a therapeutic relationship in a rehabilitation unit needs a very special spool to protect its privacy and provide sanctuary for the trust that permits the thread to be unwound, and my argument that I needed my own room to create a play therapy space I could design and control access to was accepted.

I wanted it to be a room where a child in the midst of identity loss could feel safe enough to re-connect with their past self and engage in the task of creating a new integrated sense of self, hopeful of a future and with the potential to experience post-trauma growth. There is research evidence from adults with acquired brain injury identifying that such clients need to establish a very strong sense of safety in their therapist before they are willing to process their emotions (Schoenber et al., 2006; Ashworth et al., 2011) and I worked on the premise that the same would apply for children and adolescents with brain injury.

Tragic illness or accident had robbed them of their earlier childhood trust that the world of tomorrow would be as today, and so disaster thinking reigned supreme. Their 'brilliant bodies' (the theme tune of a popular CBeebies TV programme, *Nina and the Neurons*) were brilliant no longer, and each cognitively aware child in rehabilitation lived with great anxiety. Replacing the self-esteem that accompanies a healthy functioning body was self-loathing. Replacing trust in the future was superstitious bargaining. Replacing positive emotions was a surfeit of anger, resentment, guilt, blame, jealousy, envy, bitterness, hopelessness and, crowning all, a deep fear of failure and of the humiliation and bullying it would unleash.

So the 'spool' needed to be a place of no failure, a private place quite different from the busy rehabilitation world outside the room, where adult-led agendas of nursing care, therapies and education inevitably held sway. It needed to be a place dedicated to setting free imaginative potential, because there is evidence that children with acquired brain injury can re-discover their pretend play skills and utilise the safety of symbolic distance, despite fatigue and difficulty with abstract thought (Fink et al., 2012).

I decided I would see the children twice weekly because, with so many different adults involved in their busy rehabilitation schedules, I wanted quickly to become a familiar person. As the room I was allocated could be 'spied on' through a small window in the door, I made a cartoon notice that covered that window, stating a special play session was in progress and not to disturb. Indeed, it never ceased to amaze me how salient this notice became, with even memory-impaired children reminding me to put it up if I ever forgot to do so. The auditory risk that our play and conversations might be overheard was more difficult to counter, as my room was adjacent to other therapy rooms, but by not permitting any chairs to be placed outside my door, I hoped to minimise this.

My next challenge was how to keep the room secure, because all its play resources would be on display to limit frustration for children with mobility difficulties, and the room would also contain the children's private boxes storing any craft, drawing or painting they had done. So I used another notice stating that the room was to remain locked unless in use by me.

I trawled charity shops looking for toys that would have been popular some years previously. My reasoning was that such toys would help each child to reconnect with their previous sense of self in a playful way and also support the regression in skills that accompanies long-term illness and acquired brain injury in particular. Indeed, often children would enter the room and exclaim excitedly, "I used to have one of those", and one boy said, "I've come over all tingly with happiness seeing those Sylvanian bears again". I designed the playroom to look as homely as possible, and it predominately contained toys and materials to facilitate imaginative and creative play and emotional release (Landreth, 2002)

I specifically decided there would be no disability aids or equipment to remind the children of their disabilities other than the mandatory hoist, over which I hung a colourful mobile, and the cut-out adjustable tables needed to accommodate the play of children in wheelchairs. But there were toys that had got damaged and were now mended and treasured like all the other toys, for example, a little pirate whose leg had broken off that now had a Blu-tac leg on which he was able to balance very well! Indeed such toys often became a child's favourite toy, especially if the toy's disability resonated with their own disability. As one 11-year-old boy said on surveying the room for the first time, "Oh, this is going to be my quality room".

Crucially, though, I wanted there to be no failure within this room, so there were no books to remind the children of how they used to be able to read, no jigsaws to get wrong, no board games with rules to have to follow, and after every session, each item played with was put back by me to its specific place within the room. In a residential setting where children coming for therapy know each other and each other's timetables, this was to protect confidentiality, because no child would be able to see what the previous child had been playing with. But even more imperatively, I wanted each child to experience consistency and predictability from a room that always looked the same on entering and where every item had its own place. I reasoned this would provide a deep sense of security and familiarity, feelings that facilitate emotional recovery in children living in a world beset by chaos and uncertainty (Perry and Pollard, 1998). "I just don't know why I feel so calm in here", said one

15-year-old girl, "but I just do." By arranging the room in this way, I also sought to facilitate the notion of flow, when we are so thoroughly absorbed in the here and now, using our skills to meet just achievable challenges, that time itself seems to stop (Bloom, 2010). One adolescent expressed something similar: "Why does time go so fast when I am with you?" and then with a smile, "I know, I will just have to pretend I am feeling bored and miserable and then the time will slow down!"

For each child to feel truly valued and accepted for who they now were, impaired, altered, often disfigured and changed forever, I decided I would need to offer play therapy that was highly child centred and non-directive from the moment we first met, so I decided I would not do any initial assessment with the child. I knew this would be questioned by my colleagues, who all did an initial measurable assessment as a quantifiable baseline for subsequent outcome data. Such practice is, moreover, usual now in play therapy practice driven increasingly as it is by a need to quantify outcomes to promote effective practice, but also driven increasingly by a need to release funding for play therapy in a climate governed by criteria of proven cost effectiveness from a limited and specified number of sessions.

Nevertheless I decided that for these highly challenging circumstances, where the child was engaged in such a struggle to find a new sense of self, I would need to communicate non-judgemental positive regard from the very outset of our relationship. I wanted the child only ever to know this therapeutic space as theirs, with an agenda of their own, choosing to optimise their feelings of mastery. Comments from the children like "I feel like a queen in this room, reigning over everything" bore testimony to just how far I strove to be non-directive from the very beginning (Wilson and Ryan, 2005).

Of course that did not mean that I was not assessing. From the moment the child entered the room I was indeed assessing via my own detailed and focussed observation of not only their play choices, pace and switches of play but also of their breathing pattern, their visual scanning, their degree of hyper-vigilance, their muscular tension, facial expressiveness and overall emotional regulation. Especially challenging was assessing children who had the necessary cognition to enable a therapeutic relationship to form but who had no sight or no expressive language or no ability to move any part of their body.

For such children I needed to ensure that, despite the distractions and limitations of their impairments, the child continually felt my presence and my desire to attune to their needs and desires as empathetically as I could (Ashworth et al., 2011). So I permitted myself no distractions, no paper or pen at my side to note down anything. Such self-imposed strictures meant that I could not do back-to-back sessions because I needed not only time to replace each play item to its specific place within the room but also time to jot down immediately after the session some brief notes to aid my detailed memory for my subsequent write-ups. I also needed time to read over the record of the next child's previous session so I could trace whatever linkages might occur.

Ariadne challenged

In establishing my practice along these lines, I faced challenges from my team colleagues, on grounds that it would not only be unhelpful but potentially damaging and dangerous to provide such a room for children with acquired brain injury. Their concerns were threefold: my room contained health and safety risks, quantifiable outcome measures were needed and children with acquired brain injury were highly distractible and easily overwhelmed.

Regarding the first challenge I successfully argued that my 'control measure' against health and safety risks within the room was that I would be wholly attentive to the child throughout, taking no notes during the session and being ever alert to any risk. As to the next two challenges I saw them as being inextricably linked. Gathering quantifiable outcome data necessitated measuring tools and would, I argued, compromise the high degree of child centredness I was hoping to achieve in my attempt to lower the child's anxiety. I acknowledged that acquired brain injury brings high probabilities of executive functioning impairments and behavioural symptoms of perseveration, dis-inhibition, distractibility and impulsivity (Catroppa et al., 2012). However, I argued that these symptoms were also symptoms of heightened anxiety, so if I could keep anxiety to a minimum I might be better able to isolate and identify the role being played by the organic damage (Perry and Pollard, 1998). Whatever I could do to lower anxiety through offering a playful, colourful, child-welcoming world in which the child was 'master' from the very beginning would hopefully result in children showing competencies above those they were able to show elsewhere when they were more anxious.

Although my argument was accepted and indeed subsequently evidenced, many of my colleagues remained concerned that my therapy could still overwhelm a highly distractible child. But, I counter-argued, a child-friendly, toy-cluttered environment might actually create less distractibility. The child's anxiety would be less in this non-clinical setting, and the room's predictability and consistency would prove calming once the initial stimulation of its newness had passed. So it proved to be, with even highly distractible children settling to making play choices.

But I, myself, also had concerns. How would I be able to keep to being non-directive with children in wheelchairs who needed me to reach for items, children with loss of muscular control who couldn't hold objects themselves, children with visual or auditory losses, children who could not explain to me what they wanted or what their play was all about? I knew I would so need the mantra of 'trust the child' but also need to add 'trust myself'. In the event, with the valuable benefit and support of my supervision, I was able to develop trust in the accuracy of my own acute and absorbed observation and become confident that my therapeutic alliance with the child was enabling me to sense what it was that this child wanted and that they were also finding ways to let me know when my actions and reflections did not accurately describe their choices or their feelings.

Still, with no quantifiable assessment structure in place scaffolding my intervention, my colleagues queried how it could be evidenced that my work was achieving positive outcomes? I counter-argued that I would be seeking outcome data, albeit qualitative. The children and adolescents referred to me by staff and parents, and some even self-referring, had often become demotivated by their rehabilitation programmes. Could I re-motivate them? Or the referral cited explosive anger and impulsivity. Could I help them achieve improved emotional regulation? Or the child was very frightened. Could I lessen their fright by helping them play their fears? Or the child was joyless and hopeless. Could I bring back smiles, laughter and a willingness to look forward?

There was an additional qualitative measure, however, that quickly surfaced. Even children with impaired memory wanted to know each day if they had a play therapy session. Why, staff and parents asked, did the child so eagerly anticipate their sessions of play therapy and express disappointment if told they had to wait a few days until their next session? What was the magic in a room full of old toys?

So even after just few sessions qualitative outcome data began to evidence, and it was highly supportive of an intervention that prioritised the achievement of a therapeutic relationship above all else. Other qualitative outcomes that staff and parents increasingly commented on were that the child's motivation for and engagement in their rehabilitation programme had increased during their play therapy, that their emotional regulation had improved, but above all else that their child seemed happier. As one parent said to me, "You have given me my child back; since seeing you he smiles again".

Offering the thread

Referrals came to me from both staff and parents. As mentioned earlier, I set myself a key criterion regarding referrals, that is that the child would need to evidence sufficient retained or recovered cognition to be able to form a relationship with me. So I read their medical and therapy notes carefully to confirm if this was so.

Then I made contact with parents either in person or by phone. I explained my therapy and what I hoped to achieve and took a family and brain injury history. I then sought their specific commitment to play therapy even though all therapies were covered for consent by the rehabilitation contract they had signed. There is indeed growing evidence testifying to the importance of encouraging family support if a child's recovery from brain injury is to be optimised (Anderson, Catroppa, Haritou, et al., 2005; Braga et al., 2005; Foster et al., 2012). I also checked that the referral had identified symptoms of emotional distress that were evidence based to be appropriate for play therapy intervention (Kool and Lawyer, 2010).

However, there was not only the parent's motivation for play therapy and its appropriateness to consider; there was also the need to gauge the child's motivation. So at the end of every child's first session, I asked them if they wanted to return, having first checked as best I could (especially with those children experiencing receptive language and cognitive impairments) that they had understood my explanation of play therapy as a time when I hoped some of their muddled feelings might get sorted out and where there would just be a few rules to follow to keep ourselves safe and their play choices private. All the children indicated they wanted to come back. As for determining the child's continuing motivation for play therapy and when to terminate, my usual practice was to offer sessions until the child's discharge so I could support them through the anxieties associated with this unsettling period of transition. Moreover achieving a predictable and planned ending to our relationship I knew was crucial for children who had been traumatised by loss. Only three, all of them adolescents, requested an earlier termination of their therapy.

Finally, was the child's everyday environment physically and psychologically safe enough? The children I worked with were recently traumatised, but they were not in a period of intense chaos. They were living in a safe-guarded, emotionally nurturing environment, and the appropriateness and effectiveness of play therapy in such circumstances is well documented (McMahon, 1992; Landreth, 2001).

Passages of the labyrinth

Each journey through the labyrinth, each choice of passage-way to enter, every twist and turn, whether taken by a 3-year-old or a 16-year-old as they travelled to the 'Minotaur' of their deepest worries and fears, was a unique journey. What governed their choices and their willingness, or not, to take hold of my 'thread'? Did they have secure or insecure attachment histories before sustaining their injury? Was this tragedy a discrete event in an otherwise happy childhood or yet another horror to add to a history of horrors, so they were suffering from a developmental trauma disorder (van der Kolk, 2005)? How would each of their histories impact me, and what risk of secondary trauma would I need to be alert to (Figley, 1995)?

It could take a while before the child felt ready to tackle their labyrinth. Some would play superficially at its entrance, unwilling to enter, not trusting yet that the therapeutic thread would be strong enough to keep them safe and guide them back. But once they ventured in and began to tug at the thread and I to unwind it, they traversed dark passages that I became familiar with as my caseload experience grew. The 'lair of the beast' of sudden severe acquired brain injury and the devastation and havoc that this 'beast' unleashes forms a labyrinth landscape that has key thematic characteristics.

The central passageway was one littered with 'brokenness' and 'unfairness'. Nothing would ever be the same again. The future was to be feared and deeply distrusted. The way ahead was one of rejection, a fearful fulcrum of embarrassment, teasing, humiliation and bullying. They were now 'prisoners' to their fate, damaged goods, destined never to be loved, let alone unconditionally, had that been the deep sense of belonging and acceptance they had once enjoyed.

Branching passages then beckoned. There was the passageway of guilt and self-blame for causing their parents anguish and wrecking their family's life. They had 'got ill' because they had been naughty, and this was their punishment; a child's attempt to make sense of the nonsensical. "Why did I not heed my mother's warning about crossing roads, why did I think she was a nag? Now I am being punished just for thinking that", said one boy hit by a car. Or they travelled a passageway of deep ambivalence towards their parents, parents who had not kept them safe, who, for example, had let them go on that outing where they had had their accident and suffered that severe blow to their head. Or they were angry with parents and/or doctors who had not taken their symptoms of a headache and feeling sick seriously enough, meaning their tumour had grown so big that its removal had hurt their brain in horrid ways, leaving them unable now to find the words they wanted or move in ways they had done before.

Others wanted to protect their parents and hid their distress behind false smiles. As one boy, the victim of a vicious assault, said to me, "I am Mr. Matey on that bottle of soap bubbles. Like him, I am trapped with my smile." Others had survivor guilt. Why did I survive the accident, when my parents and brother died? Then there were passages of jealousy of every able-bodied person and deep envy of siblings who were 'all right'. There was self-loathing and hatred of their altered, 'now ugly' bodies. There was the passageway of hyper-vigilance, with every sound outside the room meaning another injection was on its way, or the passageway of superstitious bargaining with the Minotaur, pleading with him to release them if they did something to placate him.

The labyrinth did however contain one prize above all else, the prize of post-traumatic growth. Should their Minotaur be beaten, should their emotional wasteland of hopelessness be vanquished, then their future could actually be enriched by having been victorious over such adversity. But would I be able to keep hold of that therapeutic thread, or would I be sorely tempted to let it go, unable to stay with the child as they journeyed deep into their labyrinth? I would need strength to manage the guilt that easily bubbled up within my 'able-bodied self' because I could not rescue the child and return them to bodily wholeness. I might feel powerless in the face of life's vagaries, finding it hard to give myself permission to live with hope rather than with dread at what the future might hold for me and those I loved. Such were my own struggles at the mouth of the maze: to stay there steadily unwinding the thread, not to flee, and to be there to greet the child when they emerged and my thread was no longer needed.

Some faces of Theseus[1]

Naomi was eight years old, an only child, registered blind since birth, and she attended 39 play therapy sessions. She arrived in the Unit 7 months after her brain injury, caused by a stroke from a blood clot that had formed following an infection. She was still experiencing right-sided weakness affecting her hand, arm and leg and she used a white stick. Fortunately her cognition and language skills had recovered well and although she had a lively intelligence and a mischievous sense of humour, she could also be challengingly oppositional and demanding. Her parents reported that she had not ever engaged in pretend play and that her play choices at home and at her special school always involved braille board games, with her favourite being Snakes and Ladders.

On entering the room Naomi asked me for Snakes and Ladders. She was disappointed when I said I did not have any board games, but that I would help her go around the room and feel what there was to choose. One cuddly toy intrigued her. She gave her a name, Betty Bunny, and said Betty was naughty and had to be thrown in the basement. When I wondered why she was being thrown away, she said Betty had been naughty so had been put in hospital and she was now rubbish. This theme surfaced again and again over Naomi's next 15 sessions, with her favourite role play being her as the doctor giving painful injections to the naughty toys and instructing me to be her helper as either a nurse or an ambulance driver.

By placing herself 'in charge' in this way she lessened her fears of intrusive medical procedures and enhanced her sense of mastery. Over the next 15 sessions the playroom became a watch factory (she wore a talking watch which was one of her most prized possessions). Naomi cast herself as the factory boss with me as her helper, but the theme of punishing the toys continued. Then peer-group rivalries between several of the cuddly toys began to surface, but now Betty Bunny was always the winner. Although a fear of rejection and bullying was a constant theme during this intermediate phase, gradually her sense of mastery strengthened. The symbolic distance she had found for processing her anxieties amazed me, especially as she had not evidenced pretend play skills previously.

In her final nine sessions Naomi's play choices became more varied. She explored other options in the room such as music making and had fun with balloons. In her final session, she chose for us to make a happy singing tape together to take home with her, an inspirational idea for a 'container' for her play therapy journey that both surprised and delighted me.

Jamie was just under three years old when he fell and sustained a severe impact injury to his brain, affecting primarily his physical abilities. When he arrived at the unit, two months later, his mobility skills were returning, and he had made a surprisingly good cognitive recovery, although his behaviour was now becoming increasingly oppositional, causing his rehabilitation progress to stall. His referral also identified that he had developed a terror of all medical intervention and that in his pretend play he was making toys fall, then screaming out and becoming very scared. He attended 21 sessions.

Jamie was extremely hyper-vigilant in his early sessions and reluctant to play. But then he found the puppets, and they became his release, providing a cathartic outlet for anger play and enabling him to experience mastery whilst playing out his fears and his frustrations. Another key theme involved the doll's house, where he made the child characters fall over and then made the adult family doll characters react with screams. In my regular meetings with his mother, I shared this theme with her, and she confirmed she let out a panicked scream even if Jamie just tripped up. I often found that 'disaster thinking' permeated parents' thoughts and reactions. This mother seemed to be suffering from this, and her response was clearly increasing her son's fearfulness, so we agreed that she should seek separate therapeutic help for herself with her own hyper-vigilance. Subsequently this theme in Jamie's play ceased. By session 12, Jamie's fears were reported by staff and parents to be lessening, his pretend play to be developing more variety and his motivation for his rehabilitation programmes increasing, enabling him to make excellent progress.

Jamie had also become better able to keep play therapy boundaries with less challenge. Towards the end of his therapy, I felt sufficiently confident in our relationship to say I could now allow him to show his favourite toy to his mummy (a little rubber sausage dressed as a football supporter who shouted out angrily if thumped) because I could trust him to bring it straight back. He not only did bring it straight back but reached up and placed it in the toy sink, which was where it lived!

Suzie was 15 years old and received 46 sessions over nine months. She arrived at the Unit 5 months after suffering a severe impact brain injury in an accident. Although her language and executive functioning skills had significantly recovered, she was in a wheelchair, still suffering from severe weakness in her left leg, paralysis in her left hand and arm, and was emotionally labile. Key worries she needed to process were anger at what had happened to her, blame towards her parents, who she held responsible for letting her go out with her friend that day, and resentment and envy of her younger sibling. She was also highly distressed about her physical impairments. Before her accident she was reported to have been disinterested in her schoolwork because, as a talented dancer, she planned to do this professionally. Her referral also identified that she was showing little motivation for her therapies, feeling everything was hopeless.

Her play choices in all her sessions were either craft based or sensory. A key theme for many weeks was finding fault with me over everything, as she was indeed doing to her mother. I was useless, I was ugly. "You have red blood in your eyes and old-looking wrinkly hands". I was "making the table messy". Projecting and transferring her distress onto me allowed us to explore themes such as her anger towards her parents, especially her mother, for not keeping her safe and her perfectionism over physical beauty, now cruelly turned into self-hatred. She set me impossible challenges so I always failed and was unable to meet her expectations. I was an endless disappointment. A key 'turning point' came when she picked up on a word I had used to help her untangle her feelings, the word *ambivalent*. "Wow", she exclaimed, "I'm going to text my friends with that one. Bet they'll be impressed". From then on she took 'twists and turns' back and forth in her labyrinth journey but emerged finally with a decision that when she was back to school she was going to concentrate on her studies. Her search for her new identity, a struggle for any adolescent, was obviously not completed whilst she was seeing me, and she left the unit with an on-going grief journey still to travel, but she had found a new direction, and some years later she did go on to university, a brave and amazing accomplishment.

Gerry was 10 years old and had sustained a traumatic brain injury four months earlier from colliding with a car whilst out cycling, breaking bones which were now mending, but more severely suffering frontal lobe brain damage to his memory, speech and executive functioning skills. At the start of his 28 sessions of play therapy, he was in a wheelchair, disorientated, highly impulsive and emotionally labile. At the time of his accident, his parents, who had acrimoniously divorced some months previously, were still locked in custody battles. Before his accident Gerry was described to have been intelligent, imaginative, caring, sensible and loving football.

This was the boy who on seeing the room for the first time said, "This is going to be my quality room". He recognised toys he had played with as a younger boy and permitting him the comfort of a 'safe' regression for his reduced skill levels. For the first few sessions he was hyper-vigilant to the tiniest noise from outside the room and even asked for the toy medical kit to be removed because it scared him. But over the coming weeks as his trust developed, he calmed and chose drawing as the main outlet for his fears. Drawing not only provided the safety of symbolic distance but also did not expose him to failure as did other play choices more reliant on executive functioning or physical skills. His right hand was uninjured, and he was able to draw whatever he liked. However, his imaginative artwork was bleak, full of weapons, body dismemberments and cruel characters. At the end of each session he would boundary challenge my rule that all work was to be kept safe, locked away in his box until the end of therapy. He wanted to show his mum and dad his drawings, but it was of course imperative that I maintained the boundary, however angry I made him. Every so often he would draw a more loving, hopeful picture.

In his final session, when allowed to choose what he wanted to stay in his box to take home with him and what he wanted destroyed, he gave every violent drawing to me, saying, "You have it, I don't need it anymore", and he just kept the few happy pictures in his box. Then he chose three white polystyrene balls from the craft box. He drew a scary face on each and put one into each of his three pockets. "These are to protect me back at school and to fight for me against the scary things".

Gerry's Minotaur had been wounded but not yet fatally. A fitting finale for me to use as an illustration to guide a therapist's expectation as to just how far a 'new sense of self' can be therapeutically nurtured within a residential rehabilitation unit, because the world outside has still to be faced.

The spool rewound

Although I have only had space for four brief vignettes, I hope they have given a glimpse into my world within the rehabilitation unit. It is a highly unique environment for a play therapist, but one I also hope that has sufficient generalisable elements to be of interest and value to all therapists working with highly traumatised children and adolescents. I prioritised relationship above all else and strove to release in the child as much a sense of mastery as possible by adopting a highly non-directive mode of therapy with no formal assessments. I created a play therapy room with minimal potential for failure or for disappointing adults and with maximal consistency, predictability and privacy in order to encourage the development of trust. I filled my room with toys and play resources that would promote a child to travel back in time as well as to envisage future possibilities.

I argued that, with respect to emotional and behavioural functioning, the organic legacy of paediatric acquired brain injury needed to be understood as potentially presenting with similar symptomology to psychologically driven heightened anxiety states. There was, therefore, an imperative to reduce anxiety as much as possible when treating such children in order to identify more accurately the causal role being played by organic injury. Injured children need to experience a language of play through which all their rehabilitation should be delivered so that they show competencies without realising they are doing so. There is undoubtedly the need for more research in all these areas, but my hope is that this chapter offers some guidelines for such research.

Ariadne's farewell

The unit was a place of challenge on so many levels, not least the personal challenge to me to tolerate the distress, to hold on to the therapeutic thread and to 'stay in the daylight' myself. For if I could not see past disaster thinking, past the existential angst of an unpredictable life to be lived in an unpredictable world, how could I weave my thread, let alone keep hold of that thread as it was pulled deep into the labyrinth?

For that strength, for the strength not to be laid low by the secondary trauma of play therapy practice in such circumstances, I owe a deep gratitude to all those who supported me at home, at work and in professional supervision. But my story is essentially one of deep respect for all the children and their families who taught me so much about survival and redemption, about seeking the holy grail of post-traumatic growth and of discovering there could be a positive and hopeful sense of self to be found, a new identity to give the confidence to begin another day.

Note

1 All names are pseudonyms and the vignettes are based on composite clinical material to protect confidentiality.

References

Anderson, V., Catroppa, C., Haritou, F., Morse, S. & Rosenfeld, J.V. (2005) Identifying Factors Contributing to Child and Family Outcome 30 Months after Traumatic Brain Injury in Children. *Journal of Neurology, Neurosurgery & Psychiatry* Vol 76 (3), 401–408.

Anderson, V., Catroppa, C., Morse, S., Haritou, F. & Rosenfeld, J. (2005) Functional Plasticity or Vulnerability after Early Brain Injury? *Pediatrics* Vol 116 (6), 1374–1382.

Ashworth, F., Gracey, F. & Gilbert, P. (2011) Compassion Focused Therapy after Traumatic Brain Injury: Theoretical Foundations and a Case Illustration. *Brain Impairment* Vol 12 (2), 128–139.

Baggerly, J. & Bratton, S. (2010) Building a Firm Foundation in Play Therapy Research: Response to Philips. *International Journal Play Therapy* Vol 19 (1), 26–38.

Bloom, C. (2010) Finding the Psychotherapeutic Harmonies Embedded within Mark Ylvisaker's Holistic Approach to Executive Function Rehabilitation. *Journal of Behavioral and Neuroscience Research* Vol 8 (1), 60–69.

Braga, L., Da Paz Junior, A. C. & Ylvisaker, M. (2005) Direct Clinician-Delivered versus Indirect Family-Supported Rehabilitation of Children with Traumatic Brain Injury: A Randomized Controlled Trial. *Brain Injury* Vol 19 (10), 819–831.

Catroppa, C., Godfrey, C., Rosenfeld, J. V., Hearps, S.J.C. & Anderson, V. (2012) Functional Recovery Ten Years after Pediatric Traumatic Brain Injury: Outcomes and Predictors. *Journal of NeuroTrauma* Vol 29 (16), 2539–2547.

Cicerone, K., Dahlberg, C., Kalmar, K., Langenbahn, D., Malec, J. & Berquist, T. (2000) Evidence-Based Cognitive Rehabilitation: Recommendations for Clinical Practice. *Archives of Physical Medicine and Rehabilitation* Vol 81 (12), 1596–1615.

Collicutt McGrath, J. (2011) Posttraumatic Growth and Spirituality after Brain Injury. *Brain Impairment* Vol 12 (2), 82–92.

Figley, C. R. (1995) *Compassion Fatigue: Coping with Secondary Traumatic Stress Disorder in Those Who Treat the Traumatized.* Bristol: Brunner/Mazel.

Fink, N., Stagnitti, K. & Galvin, J. (2012) Pretend Play of Children with Acquired Brain Injury: An Exploratory Study. *Developmental Neurorehabilitation* Vol 15 (5), 336–342.

Foster, A., Armstrong, J., Buckley, A., Sherry, J., Young, T., Foliaki, S., James-Hohaia, T. M., Theadom, A. & McPherson, K. (2012) Encouraging Family Engagement in the Rehabilitation Process: A Rehabilitation Provider's Development of Support Strategies for Family Members of People with Traumatic Brain Injury. *Disability and Rehabilitation* Vol 34 (22), 1855–1862.

Greenfield, S. (1998) *The Human Brain: A Guided Tour.* London: Phoenix.

Harter, S. (1999) *The Construction of Self: A Developmental Perspective.* New York: Guilford Press.

Jones, E. M. & Landreth, G. (2002) The Efficacy of Individual Play Therapy for Chronically Ill Children. *International Journal of Play Therapy* Vol 11 (1), 117–140.

Kool, R., & Lawyer, T. (2010) Play Therapy: Considerations and Applications for the Practitioner. *Psychiatry (Edgmont)* Vol 7 (10), 19–24.

Landreth, G. (ed.) (2001) *Innovations in Play Therapy: Issues, Process and Special Populations.* Hove: Brunner-Routledge.

Landreth, G. (2002) *Play Therapy: The Art of the Relationship* (2nd ed.). Hove: Brunner-Routledge.

Lennon, A., Bramham, J., Carroll, A., McElligott, J., Carton, C., Waldron, B., Fortune, D., Burke, T., Fitzhenry, M. & Benson, C. (2014) A Qualitative Exploration of How Individuals Reconstruct Their Sense of Self Following Acquired Brain Injury in Comparison with Spinal Cord Injury. *Brain Injury* Vol 28 (1), 27–37.

McMahon, L. (1992) *The Handbook of Play Therapy.* London: Routledge.

Muenchberger, H., Kendall, E. & Neal, R. (2008) Identity Transition Following Traumatic Brain Injury: A Dynamic Process of Contraction, Expansion and Tentative Balance. *Brain Injury* Vol 22 (12), 979–992.

Perry, B. & Pollard, R. (1998) Homeostasis, Stress, Trauma, and Adaptation: A Neurodevelopmental View of Childhood Trauma. *Child and Adolescent Psychiatric Clinics of North America* Vol 7 (1), 33–51.

Ray, S., Schottelkorb, A. & Tsai, M. (2007) Play Therapy with Children Exhibiting Symptoms of Attention Deficit Hyperactivity Disorder. *International Journal of Play Therapy* Vol 16 (2), 95–111.

Schoenber, M., Hulme, F., Zeeman, P. & Teasdale, T. W. (2006) Working Alliance and Patient Compliance in Brain Injury Rehabilitation, and Their Relation to Psychosocial Outcome. *Journal of Neuropsychological Rehabilitation* Vol 16 (3), 298–314.

Sunderland, M. (2006) *What Every Parent Needs to Know*. London: Dorling Kindersley.

van der Kolk, B.A. (2005) Developmental Trauma Disorder. *Psychiatric Annals* Vol 35 (5), 401–408.

Webb, P. (2001) Play Therapy with Traumatized Children: A Crisis Response. In Landreth, G. (ed) *Innovations in Play Therapy: Issues, Process, and Special Populations*, pp. 289–302. Hove: Brunner-Routledge.

Wilson, K., & Ryan, V. (2005) *A Non-Directive Approach for Children and Adolescents* 2nd Edn. Oxford: Balliere Tindall.

Ylvisaker, M. (ed.) (1998) *Traumatic Brain Injury Rehabilitation: Children and Adolescents* (2nd ed.). Newton, MA: Butterworth-Heinemann.

Zimmer, C. (2014) Secrets of the Brain. *National Geographic* Vol 225 (2), 36–57.

Chapter 7

Tackling taboos

Research in play therapy

Paula Reed

Introduction

There is something intrinsically un-playful about the notion of research, and for therapists who value the role of play in communication and expression, research can seem uninspiring. Nevertheless, research is necessary to bring the value of play therapy to a wider audience and demonstrate its worthy place amongst therapeutic options for children.[1] Without the necessary research, play therapy processes remain intangible and elusive. This is particularly challenging because of the range of communications within play therapy that are essentially non-verbal.

In this chapter I ask a number of questions: What do we mean by play therapy? What differentiates it from other forms of therapy? What do we mean by play therapy research? I outline some of what I see as the challenges faced by play therapists undertaking research and researchers interested in play therapy. I discuss some of the structural barriers to conceiving and carrying out research in play therapy and explore challenges that relate to adopting and developing research approaches consistent with the values and practices of play therapy. I also discuss some of the possibilities for qualitative, quantitative, process and outcome-oriented research.

In the second half of the chapter I describe some research into the applicability of a validated measure, namely the Child Psychotherapy Q-Set (CPQ: Schneider and Jones, 2004), to play therapy. This measure offers a way of delineating play therapy from other therapeutic approaches and of developing a characteristic prototype to be used in research studies, including those that include qualitative measures.

Finally I encourage play therapists to put their creative minds to innovate ways of researching the important approach that is play therapy and for others to turn their minds to re-evaluating what valid 'research' means and what constitutes fitting data. I hope this chapter will be of interest to play therapists and students as they tussle with the complexities of undertaking research in play therapy.

What is play therapy?

To undertake research in play therapy, we need to be able to define what play therapy *is* as well as to articulate the theory and philosophy that underpins the approach. For the purposes of this chapter, it is necessary to first look at the definition(s) of play therapy and its origins.

Play therapy is defined as a "means of creating intense relationship experiences between therapist and children or young people in which play is the principal medium of communication" (Wilson and Ryan, 2000: 3). The British Association of Play Therapists (2015) defines play therapy as "a way of helping children express their feelings and deal with their emotional problems, using play as the main communication tool" (BAPT definition, 2015). These are broad definitions and are inclusive of a range of theoretical approaches.

Play therapy in the UK emerged partly from the work of Melanie Klein and Anna Freud who, in their work analysing children, used play in recognition of the restrictions of verbal interactions with young children. However, the model of play therapy taught and practised by the British Association of Play Therapists (BAPT) is one that is influenced by humanistic psychology and specifically by person-centred therapy developed by Carl Rogers (1990). Virginia Axline, who was herself a student of Carl Rogers, developed an approach to working thera-peutically with children that was defined by these principles and which Axline described in her account of a child who she named Dibs (Axline, 1964). It was from this work that the non-directive approach now known as child-centred play therapy (CCPT) emerged.

Rather than using play as an 'intervention' for the purposes of an assessment or to better communicate information to the child, such as prior to medical pro-cedures, CCPT emphasises a philosophically determined therapeutic approach to working with children: "(it) is an attitude, a philosophy and a way of being with children rather than a way of doing something to, or for, children" (Lan-dreth, 2002: 60). Play makes mutuality possible within the therapeutic relation-ship (Frankel, 1998), and it is the relationship that is considered essential to the therapy process and therapeutic change. The fundamental belief in the approach is that the child leads the way (Van Fleet et al., 2010) and that children, like all people, have the ability to self-heal given the necessary conditions to do so. In the UK, BAPT play therapists aspire to the "core conditions", defined by Rogers (1990) as empathy, unconditional positive regard and congruence. These qualities are considered fundamental to the therapeutic relationship between therapist and child. The aims of therapy are to bring about changes in close relationships and to bring the child's emotional and social functioning level with their develop-mental stage. Child-centred play therapy shares with other approaches a focus on the therapist–child relationship and the inner experiences of the child (Cochran et al., 2010). However, unlike in some other therapeutic approaches to working with children, namely classical psychoanalytic modalities, a child-centred play therapist does not interpret back to the child his or her play but keeps the play 'in the metaphor', not challenging the symbolism of the child's play. The therapist engages the child in their play, and difficult feelings are expressed and safety maintained by symbolic distance.

Play is inherently therapeutic, and it allows for "greater curiosity, exploration, spontaneity, novel behaviour and creativity", as well as the "renegotiation of self–other relationships through action" (Frankel, 1998: 150). The subtleties of expression that are out of reach for many children in verbal communication can be communicated through play. In pretend play, the child straddles the two worlds of internal and external realities, bridging the perceptual and the imaginary. The 'characters' the child brings to the play are aspects of themselves that they have not been able to come to terms with or the parts that "do not seem to mesh well with other people" (Frankel, 1998: 152). The therapist needs to be attuned to the child and attend to his[2] communications as a "total activity" (Ryan and Wilson, 2000: 54). Dissociated self-states can be expressed symbolically through their enactment or through projective play. In play therapy, the therapist joins with the child to co-construct the play in a way that "elevates the process of creativity, and therefore transformation, and does not pretend to be able to reduce its meaning to something that can be captured by words" (Frankel, 1998: 164).

Play therapy and research

Play therapy struggles to define itself as a discrete and valid discipline. Evidence-based practice and empirical research that is able to demonstrate effectiveness, as well as communicate to play therapists and across to other disciplines, is essential if play therapists are to establish play therapy as both compelling and legitimate. However, methods of inquiry must be consistent with the values and practices of play therapy rather than blindly imported from other disciplines. Research and practice need to be integrated with a commitment to develop a bottom-up rather than top-down approach where innovations emerge from practice (McLeod, 2001).

To date there appear to be two drivers for research into play therapy. One is the crucial need to demonstrate play therapy's effectiveness in promoting positive change in children, namely outcome research. This is not only for the requirements of funding bodies or therapists but also for the children who are set to benefit. The other is the need to establish a way to describe and make visible the *therapeutic process* of play therapy. Traditionally this split in research attitudes has been one between quantitative (outcome-oriented) and qualitative (process-oriented) methodologies. However, it can be helpful to think about research along continuums and placed within one of four quadrants (Figure 7.1).

The body of research that asserts the effectiveness of play therapy is based largely upon quantitative outcome measures. Bratton and Ray (2000) undertook a comprehensive literature review of 82 play therapy research studies from 1942 onwards. They identified 82 papers reporting 'experimental' research that

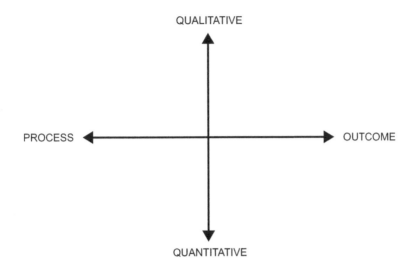

QUALITATIVE

PROCESS ⟵――――――――――――⟶ OUTCOME

QUANTITATIVE

Figure 7.1 Research methodology dimensions

included play therapy as the 'intervention' as well as pre and post measures. The authors state that the majority of the studies reviewed "identified treatment as non-directive play therapy" but note the "lack of description of play therapy procedures (the process) represents a weakness in the research" (Bratton and Ray, 2000: 50). Nevertheless they argue that their wide-ranging review demonstrates the effectiveness of play therapy in treating children with a range of problems identified in the studies. In a later meta-analysis (Bratton et al., 2005) of 93 outcome studies, the authors point to a need for training and adherence to protocol and treatment integrity in research. They note that for lasting benefit play therapy is likely to be required for longer than usually provided in 'managed care' and suggest that parental involvement is likely to have a positive influence. They assert that play therapy is "uniquely responsive to the developmental needs of children" (Bratton et al., 2005: 385). In the United Kingdom, a systematic scoping review of the evidence and effectiveness of counselling and psychotherapy with children and young people (2013) noted the increase in studies demonstrating the effectiveness of play therapy. However, all the studies cited originated in the United States, demonstrating the dearth of systematic research into the efficacy of play therapy in the UK.

Thus, elevating the credibility of play therapy through research has been based largely upon outcome measures in the United States (Reddy et al., 2005). The Association for Play Therapy (APT), in the United States, has developed a research strategy founded upon experimental outcome studies involving the application of play therapy for specific issues (Baggerley and Bratton, 2010). Urquiza (2010) argues that the randomised control trial (RCT) provides the strongest scientific and causal evidence that a specific psychotherapy approach is effective. The RCT is the gold standard of clinical research and is based upon group-focused, quantitative analyses (McLeod, 2001). Researchers in the United States (Ray, 2011) now promote manualised play therapy interventions. This follows a trend in the United States to produce brand-name treatments. However, manualised interventions do not enlarge on the process of therapy and, therefore, precisely what it is that produces therapeutic change is unavailable to scrutiny. The use of manuals assumes that it is possible to replicate an intervention and considers the therapist and child to be constants rather than variables. Goodman (2010a: 38) is particularly critical: "The human relationship therefore, becomes mechanised for the sake of science . . . both bad psychotherapy and bad science".

Likewise, Phillips (2010), in his critique of play therapy research, is critical of the lack of homogeneity of cases, approaches, measures and methods in the meta-analysis of outcome research studies. In response to some of these concerns, there has been a concerted effort amongst researchers to be much clearer about their criteria for inclusion in studies (Ray and Schottelkorb, 2010). However, this strict control of who is included in RCTs does not account for complexity or coexisting pathologies that are often characteristic of children who are referred for therapy. A closer look at the evidence reveals a frustrating lack of detail on the play therapy process and what it is that is most effective.

Outcome measures

A great deal of play therapy research has become directly associated with outcome studies, seeking to answer the questions 'Does it work?' and, if so, 'Does it work better, and more cheaply than other therapeutic interventions with children?' Some play therapists who work in organisations may be involved in outcome studies and measures to assess outcomes, which are often borrowed from other disciplines and approaches and may or may not be transferable to play therapy.

The outcome measures used as part of trials are themselves not without problem. To date, the more commonly used outcome measures quantify behaviours and the impact the child's behaviours have on the lives of adults around them, for example, the *Strengths and Difficulties Questionnaire* (Goodman, 1997) and the *Child Behaviour Checklist* (Achenbach, 1991). Studies frequently rely upon the views of third-party participants, for example parents/carers and teachers and their interpretations of changed behaviours as indications of progress (or compliance). There are discrepancies according to the theoretical orientation of therapists in what constitutes a positive outcome. Psychodynamic approaches value the conscious interpretation and verbal insights as indicators of therapeutic change. In CCPT benefit can be achieved without the children necessarily displaying conscious understanding of these processes through verbalisation. Outcome measures, on the whole, do not measure changes in the internal worlds of children or their subjective experiences of their well-being. This colludes with the power imbalance between child and adult and runs counter to the mutuality of the therapeutic relationship strived for in CCPT. All this begs the question of what we really mean by 'success' in therapy.

Process research

Process research is important because it can describe what play therapists *do*. For outcome measures to be meaningful, we need to be able to describe process: what we are doing that leads to the outcome. This is important if we are to be able to describe play therapy as a discrete approach. Process research is defined by Kennedy and Midgley (2007: 8) as the empirical study of "*why* and *how* change takes place as the consequence of a therapeutic intervention". Without a better understanding of the processes or mechanisms through which therapy operates, progress will be impaired. Process research is a way of acknowledging the complexities and subtleties that are inherent in therapy by attempting to understand both the moment-by-moment nuances as well as the intervention in its entirety. Elliot (2012: 71) describes a broad orienting framework of the change process involving the processes of the therapist, the client and the relational as well as the contexts and the effects of change. Therefore, to fully explicate outcomes, there is a requirement to expound and understand the process of play therapy and what it is that leads to change.

By looking qualitatively at what actually happens in play therapy, such as the identification of pivotal therapeutic events (Harvey, 2011), the interaction between child and play therapist (Carroll, 2005) and attention to changes in play behaviours (Ryan and Edge, 2012), we can better understand how what occurs within play therapy translates to outcomes. Nevertheless, there is a relative neglect in the literature about the quality of the therapeutic relationship in play therapy, despite the recognition of the relationship being fundamental to the outcome of therapy (Crenshaw and Kenney-Noziska, 2014). This can be attributed in part to the pressures for quick therapeutic results putting greater emphasis on the tools of the trade and away from the therapeutic process and relationship. The pursuit of "breakthrough techniques" (Crenshaw and Kenney-Noziska, 2014: 34) can threaten to distort the therapeutic process away from one that honours the child's journey to emotional safety and trust and the therapist's resolve to be therapeutically present for the child. Play therapy research (as with a good deal of counselling and psychotherapy research) is different from research in medical and pharmaceutical industries, in which breakthroughs are made in laboratories and tested in the field. In play therapy research, innovations are likely to emerge from practice (McLeod, 2001). A body of research and theory-building spirals from the interplay of practice, research and the integration of knowledge as it develops in cognate disciplines. However, without a clearer articulation and adherence to child-centred/non-directive play therapy, the door is left open to a proliferation of techniques that lack empirical support and conceptual clarity.

Qualitative research

Within the arts therapies, qualitative approaches to research are considered congruent with the way arts, including play, therapists see the world and engage with it (Barham, 2003). Qualitative approaches add depth and meaning to the data and can contribute insights to process and are argued to be most appropriate for exploring play therapy, especially the therapeutic process and relationship (Glazer and Stein, 2010). Glazer and Stein (2010: 55) state that "qualitative research is a natural extension of the therapeutic process". They comment on the shared position of relating to participants with unconditional positive regard, empathy and congruence. They uphold the values of more qualitative approaches that place meaning and intersubjectivity as central to the research inquiry. They discuss a number of methodological approaches situated within the family of qualitative inquiry, namely grounded theory, hermeneutics and phenomenology.

Qualitative approaches to research can provide a way to focus upon the "experience as well as the effect" (Daniel-McKeigue, 2006: 25). Individual case studies have employed additional qualitative analyses that contribute to theory generation (Ryan and Needham, 2001; Josefi and Ryan, 2004; Snow et al., 2009). The case study has been used for many years to elaborate on the theoretical, diagnostic and clinical bases of psychoanalytic therapy. As such it provides a 'narrative canvas' that is arguably a more accurate account of therapeutic encounter than information yielded from experimental design (Goodman, 2010a: 22). The evidence or data for these approaches is "the transcript produced from the dialogue – from the recollection, reflection and interpretation of the encounter" (Glazer and Stein, 2010: 55). This allows for a rich and interpretative analysis. However the traditional case study, because of its reliance on language and, more precisely dialogue, is a weakness as it pertains to play therapy research. One of the fundamental and defining characteristics of play therapy is that it does not rely on words. As discussed earlier, it is a child-centred approach in which the play therapist responds to however the child chooses to communicate, whether it be via play in its widest sense, through the use of language or via non-verbal communication. Any analysis of a 'transcript' needs to be able to capture this. Moreover, the case study can become a vehicle to show off the brilliance of the therapist whilst the equally valid findings and discussion of what does not work or when an intervention fails are less likely to be published (Goodman, 2010a).

Structural issues and play therapy research

There are other structural issues that impact the opportunities for research into play therapy. In the United Kingdom, the vast majority of play therapists are primarily practitioners. Only a handful of therapists have roles within universities and are active researchers. Access to academic libraries and ethics committees is restricted, and academic communities are limited. For play therapists interested in pursuing research, PhD study is an option, but currently there is no framework for academic/research career progression on completion of a doctoral thesis and a dearth of play therapists available to supervise at doctoral level. The limited play therapy research that does get published appears in specialist play therapy journals rather in than the child and adolescent psychology journals and books that are read by a wider audience (McLaughlin et al., 2013).

Play therapy concerns children, and yet a disproportionate number of the research papers are about the experiences of adults, either the parents or professionals, and about play therapy as an approach. There may be a variety of reasons for this, but one is undoubtedly the fact that research with children is fraught with challenges. There are some practical issues with regard to research with children, for example finding appropriate settings and informed consent and obtaining ethics clearance to undertake research with vulnerable children, all of which can present major hurdles. Acknowledgment and discussion of the ethics of involving children in play therapy research is scant in the play therapy literature (see Alderson and Morrow, 2011, for a thorough exploration of the topic).

However, as play therapists who are committed to play therapy and believe in its value to not only 'make children feel better' but also hear their voices and understand their worlds, we surely have an obligation to bring something of play therapy to a wider audience. Impatient to demonstrate the value of play therapy, play therapists can feel overwhelmed by the magnitude of what lies before them. However, proof of the efficacy of play therapy will not be determined by one study using one perfect instrument. Such a study or instrument does not exist, and play therapists need to recognise that evidence-based research and practice take a long time to develop using small steps.

Moreover, rather than continually reinventing the wheel, play therapy researchers can look to other therapeutic approaches where research is more developed, such as in psychoanalytic psychotherapy. It may be that instruments can be shared to describe therapeutic processes of different modalities and pooled to better inform the growing evidence of "what works for whom" (Fonagy et al., 2002). If we can describe process in a shared language and we can identify what play therapy 'looks like' as opposed, for instance, to cognitive behavioural therapy, then we can make better sense of outcome measures. As we can get a better sense of what it is that is working, we can then start to elaborate on the more nuanced play therapy processes with elegant bespoke qualitative approaches to build a multidimensional and holistic account of play therapy.

The Child Psychotherapy Q-Set

The second half of this chapter describes a study (Reed, 2012) designed to assess the relevance of the Child Psychotherapy Q-Set (CPQ; Schneider and Jones, 2004) to play therapy. The purpose of this study was twofold:

- To determine the applicability of this validated instrument of 100 qualitative items using Q-sort methodology to describe therapist, child and interactional processes within play therapy.
- To identify a characteristic prototype for play therapy as it is practised by qualified play therapists ($n = 24$) that could then be used to contrast the

approach with other modalities such as cognitive behavioural therapy and psychodynamic therapy with existing CPQ prototypes.

The CPQ (Schneider and Jones, 2004) is designed to be relevant across therapeutic modalities and is achieving recognition from child psychoanalytic psychotherapy (PDT) and cognitive behavioural therapy (CBT) as a way of describing and understanding process. The CPQ is an essentially *quantitative* measure, but its use of *qualitative* items enables description of *process* in a 'fine grained way' (Schneider et al., 2010).

The CPQ is a validated instrument that offers a systematic means of describing the complexities of the therapist–child interaction in a meaningful way (Schneider et al., 2010) that can then be *related to outcome* measures. The CPQ is used to explore the process of child psychotherapy with children aged between 3 and 13 years old. It is pan-theoretical and appropriate as a clinical research tool across a range of theoretical approaches to therapy with children. As such, it is written in 'basic language' in order to assess the therapeutic process across and between theoretical schools (Schneider et al., 2010). It has been designed to "provide a language and rating procedure for describing and researching the therapeutic process in clinically relevant terms in a form suitable for quantitative comparison and analysis" (Anna Freud Centre, 2011). To date it has been used primarily in psychoanalytic child psychotherapy (Bambery et al., 2007; Schneider et al., 2010), but also with cognitive behavioural therapy (Schneider et al., 2009). Prior to this study, the CPQ had not been used within play therapy[3] (Schneider, 2011).

The CPQ consists of 100 qualitative statements, or items, and is used to analyse video-recorded sessions of therapy with children. By using qualitative items, it seeks to represent "the richness, complexity and continuity of entire sessions" (Schneider et al., 2010: 95) rather than the strict operationalising of moment-to-moment behaviours of the therapist and child. Nevertheless, the CPQ offers a way of making tangible some of the more elusive moments in therapy. The CPQ can be used as a standalone measure or used in combination with other methods.

The CPQ is designed to provide a way of comparing and contrasting therapies, therapists and different variables in the therapeutic encounter. It was devised to identify what elements in the process of therapy promote change and which hinder it (Schneider et al., 2010). It offers a way of understanding and conceptualising the process of play therapy before attempting to explicate outcomes. The complete set of items in the CPQ represents a range of child and therapist characteristics (Schneider, 2004):

- Items that describe the child's attitudes, feelings, behaviour and experience
- Items that reflect the therapist's actions and attitudes
- Items that attempt to capture the nature or atmosphere of the session

The method is unobtrusive in that it uses video recordings of sessions that are rated subsequently.

Q methodology

The Child Psychotherapy Q-Set is designed to be used as a Q-sort. Q methodology is used as a general scaling technique to provide convenient ways of organising data in terms of how it describes a particular construct, person or situation. The Q-sort has similarities with Likert scaling but is a 'forced-choice' method, requiring the rater to select one item in relation to another. It is 'ipsative', in that it requires raters to sort items in terms of the degree to which they are 'characteristic' or 'not characteristic' of the construct, person or situation being described. In the CPQ, the Q-sort relates to the whole session and seeks to capture some of the complexities of therapy.

During rating, the material is studied, and the 100 items, written on cards, are sorted into one of nine categories. A fixed number of items are placed at each of the nine categories from 'not at all characteristic' to 'highly characteristic'. So, for example, if item 76 of the CPQ, "Therapist makes links between child's feelings and experience", is considered characteristic of the therapy session observed, then that card would be placed with those items considered to be 'most characteristic' to the material, towards the right-hand side, whilst those items considered to be 'least characteristic' are placed towards the left (see Figure 7.2).

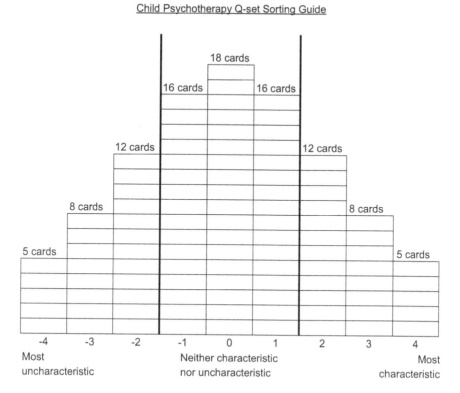

Child Psychotherapy Q-set Sorting Guide

Figure 7.2 Child Psychotherapy Q-Set pattern

The forced sorting in Q-sort requires raters to place the items following a specified distribution of 5, 8, 12, 16, 18, 16, 12, 8, 5 cards. This formation represents the bell-shaped curve of normative distribution. This process forces the rater to think comparatively, in other words to rate the item in comparison to the other 99 items. The forced distribution of the Q-sort into a normative pattern of distribution differentiates it from a Likert scale. Once Q-sorted, and provided data are sufficient, the data are amenable to parametric statistical analyses.

Of course, even with 100 items, it is somewhat of a compromise, but nevertheless it provides a way of considering a session in its entirety, with the forced-choice method producing a spider's web of interconnected items. All 100 items need to be included, as the structure of the analysis is dependent upon all items and their relationship to one another. Over time these interrelationships between items are used to identify "interaction structures" (Goodman, 2010a). Items placed centrally reflect their relative neutrality or unimportance in relation to the other items. From this the *relative* importance of qualitative items in one session can be identified and, when repeated across sessions, extrapolated to provide a "motion portrait" of therapy (Schneider et al., 2010: 99).

An advantage of the CPQ is that it is designed to be unobtrusive and relies upon video recording, thereby not unduly influencing the process. The data used in the CPQ reflects the session as a whole whilst providing a fine-grained analysis. It is designed to fit therapy, as it occurs naturalistically, rather than changing therapy to meet the demands of research. In addition, it is a child-friendly instrument in that it is designed to take into account all the communications of the child and therapist and does not rely solely on verbal communication. For these reasons, it lends itself to the non-intrusive child-centred approach of play therapy. Ethical consideration for the CPQ-sort involves primarily informed consent and the viewing and storage of video recordings.

In order to establish the applicability of the CPQ to play therapy and to determine if a Q-sort prototype characteristic of play therapy could be discerned, I undertook a small-scale project. This used the responses of BAPT–qualified and experienced play therapists (Reed, 2012). Since the inception of the CPQ, a number of *prototypes*, or profiles, of a *typical therapeutic encounter* from differing modalities have been developed. This offers a way of comparing and contrasting different approaches and contributes to our overall understanding of what works for whom. To first establish the perceived 'fit' of the CPQ to play therapy the tool was sent, in questionnaire form, to 'expert' play therapists for their assessment of the appropriateness of the CPQ and to develop a characteristic profile of play therapy.

The method used replicated earlier work done to establish an empirical foundation for the differences and similarities of different therapeutic modalities with children, undertaken as part of the development of the CPQ (Schneider, 2004). It was anticipated that the resultant profile could then be used to compare and contrast the play therapy prototype with other existing prototypes (Schneider, 2004; Bambery et al., 2007; Schneider et al., 2009). Ultimately, this analysis could then build on a picture of what makes for effective therapy with children and what distinguishes play therapy from other interventions. In addition, the acceptability and perceived appropriateness of the CPQ by the play therapist respondents could be assessed and potential applications for both practice and further research explored.

Potential participants were identified from the British Association of Play Therapists (BAPT) via email and invited to enrol in the study and to receive the questionnaire and explanatory notes. The explanatory notes outlined the purpose of the study and asked the respondent to indicate on a nine-point Likert scale to what degree each of the 100 items of the CPQ were characteristic of an 'ideal', or what they considered to be a typical, play therapy session, according to the principles of their theoretical orientation. The scale was labelled –4, most uncharacteristic, to +4, most characteristic, with 0 being the neutral point. In addition, the respondents were asked about their training, theoretical base and professional experience. The play therapists were also given the opportunity to give more qualitative feedback on the CPQ and its perceived applicability to play therapy.

This approach was first piloted on four expert play therapists to ensure clarity of the task and make revisions as necessary. To replicate earlier studies with different therapeutic approaches, a target of 30 participants was set, as this number also allows for statistical analysis. The expert play therapists were approached indirectly via email, and their inclusion in the study was on an 'opt in' basis, with responses anonymised.

The quantitative data from the scaling exercise and the qualitative data from their written responses were collated. The ratings according to the Likert scale were entered onto an SPSS Statistics 19 database and analysed for the 24 play therapy respondents. A single prototype distribution for play therapy was composited using SPSS 19 and two-tailed ANOVA. This showed the mean ratings for each item across the respondents and the most and the least salient items. As the play therapists' ratings did not follow the forced normal distribution usually applied to Q-sort ratings, these were recoded and Spearman's Rank Correlation Coefficient used for correlational comparisons.

The resultant play therapy prototype was compared to existing prototypes for psychodynamic and cognitive behavioural prototypes (Schneider et al., 2009). The mean ratings were calculated and correlated with the mean ratings for psychodynamic child psychotherapy and cognitive behavioural therapy with children as described previously (Schneider, 2004; Schneider et al., 2009). This was undertaken with the assistance of Professor Geoff Goodman at Long Island University, New York.

The qualitative data comprising feedback on the instrument and details about the theoretical orientation and experience of the respondent, as well as emailed feedback on the process, were analysed using thematic analysis (Joffe, 2012). During the analysis, points raised by respondents were taken back to the author of the instrument and one of the co-trainers on the CPQ training for their views.

The respondents

Of the 243 play therapists contacted, 31 replied, and 24 sets of data were returned (9.9% response rate). The majority described their approach as child centred and/ or non-directive and had been practising between 2.5 and 22 years as a play thera- pist. The play therapists worked with children experiencing a range of difficulties in a variety of settings.

Qualitative data

The analysis of the qualitative data revealed that 48% of respondents considered the CPQ set to be a usable measure and appropriate to play therapy. Comments included, "Thought provoking and relevant" and, from another respondent, "I think these statements are very relevant to my play therapy practice". Another 46% of respondents included both positive and negative elements. Some respon- dents commented on the process and their difficulty in conceiving a typical play therapy session, when play therapy can be so different from one child and situa- tion to the next. They commented that it was easier to respond to items concerning the attitude of the therapist than the behaviours of the child.

For the purpose of distinguishing a prototype, the respondents were asked to report on the questionnaire without applying it to an actual session. It was a chal- lenge to respond to the instrument 'in the abstract', although some were able to recognise a potential for its use in practice: " . . . if I was using the questionnaire to explore my work with a specific child it would certainly be relevant. It was quite hard to answer in the abstract though" (child-centred and non-directive play therapist).

Some respondents (four) identified a lack of emphasis on the use of the meta- phor and symbolic play in therapy with children: "It was difficult to find relevance in some questions because they did not easily allow the awareness of the meta- phor or symbolic play". This was seen as central to their work in facilitating a safe and contained exploration through symbolic distance.

Respondents (two) perceived an emphasis on direct verbal communication that they considered less appropriate for therapy with very young children or those with disabilities. One respondent felt that more could be included on the characteristics of the therapist. For example, 'playfulness' was seen as a quality that was sometimes used in therapy and, by implication, more apparent in play therapy.

Some respondents commented on how the context of the therapy could influ- ence play therapy and their way of working with a child. Sessions could be limited to a fixed number in some organisations, and the greater or lesser involvement of family were not reflected in the instrument. Only one respondent saw no relevance in the instrument.

Quantitative data

Once the ratings according to a Likert scale were analysed for the 24 play therapy respondents, they were composited into a single prototype distribution. From this prototype the most salient characteristics and the least salient characteristics from the composite of the twenty-four questionnaires could be identified using SPSS (see Table 7.1). There was very good concordance for the 'most salient' characteristics and good concordance for the 10 'least salient' points.

Below are the ten 'most salient' from a choice of 100 items:

Table 7.1 The most and least characteristic items of the play therapy prototype

Most salient

Item 6: The therapist is sensitive to the child's feelings
Item 77: The therapist's interaction with the child is sensitive to the child's level of development
Item 52: The therapist makes explicit statements about the end of the hour, upcoming weekend or holiday
Item 75: Interruptions, breaks in treatment or termination of therapy are discussed
Item 48: Therapist sets limits
Item 45: Therapist tolerates child's strong affects and impulses
Item 71: Child engages in make believe play
Item 28: Therapist accurately perceives the therapeutic process
Item 4: There is discussion why the child is in therapy
Item 65: Therapist clarifies, restates or rephrases child's communication.

And the 'least salient points':

Item 55: Therapist directly rewards desirable behaviours
Item 9: Therapist is nonresponsive v. actively engaged
Item 18: Therapist is judgmental and conveys lack of acceptance
Item 24: Therapist's emotional conflicts intrude into the relationship
Item 21: Therapist self discloses
Item 41: Child does not feel understood by therapist
Item 5: Child has difficulty understanding the therapist's comments
Item 37: Therapist behaves in a didactic manner
Item 17: Therapist actively asserts control over the interaction (e.g. structuring, introducing new topics)
Item 66: Therapist is directly reassuring

Least salient

On close inspection of all the data it is apparent that some of the more neutrally placed items, represent a much greater discrepancy in responses than others. So for some items respondents thought they were extremely characteristic, while others thought the same item was uncharacteristic. For example, item 31, "therapy session has a focus or a theme", attracted a wide range of responses despite an average rating of 0. It may be worth looking at some of these items more carefully and could provide the focus of further delineation of the play therapy prototype.

Once the play therapy CPQ prototype was defined, it was compared to existing prototypes for psychodynamic and cognitive behavioural prototypes, held by Geoff Goodman at Long Island University, New York State. The play therapy prototype was highly correlated with the psychodynamic prototype (.75) and non-significantly correlated to the cognitive behavioural therapy prototype (.135).

Discussion

The process of collating the responses and using them to create a profile of the way play therapists practise also provides an enlightening insight into the similarities and differences in their ways of working. Despite being able to identify the most salient and the least salient points with some confidence, there was considerable variation in response to other items.

The BAPT acknowledges that "Play Therapy encompasses many approaches but the foundation of all approaches is child-centred" and it "promotes person-centred therapy based on humanistic principles" (BAPT, 2015). Despite the development of a characteristic profile reflecting a coherent model of play therapy, the data highlighted considerable variation of theoretical position. This variance was reflected in the analysis of the questionnaires when evolving the prototype.

There may be a number of reasons for these differences:

- The instrument is designed to be used by therapists and/or researchers after training in the use of the CPQ (Midgley, 2012, personal correspondence). Therefore, despite the explanatory notes, respondents may have interpreted the questions inaccurately.
- Some of the items, when considered in the abstract, based upon a 'characteristic session', may be difficult to agree upon. This was also expressed as a challenge in the development of the PDQ prototype.
- There is a lack of homogeneity of theoretical approach and application by BAPT play therapists.

This last point perhaps requires further investigation. If such variance cannot be accounted for by points 1 and 2, then it suggests that there is variation in approach. Incoherence of approach is problematic if play therapy is to become established as a discrete theoretically and evidence-based therapeutic modality. Phillips (1985) describes play therapy as it is practised in the United States by stating that it covers a variety of clinical theories and interventions that warrant more careful elucidation. The CPQ-sort offers a validated way of doing just this. Further development of a prototype, with a larger sample, could lead to a tighter model of play therapy as it is practised by BAPT play therapists. Video-recorded sessions can be compared to the prototype for play therapy to assess theoretical adherence over time. This would improve internal as well as discriminant validity of the prototype.

For the individual researcher using the CPQ as a way of describing process in single-case studies, this variance from the prototype in itself is not a concern. The CPQ-sort can measure and illustrate changes in the child, the therapist and the relationship across the course of therapy where the child and therapist remain 'constant'. Variance becomes problematic where outcome studies are based on an assumption of sameness, as for example in manualised treatments. This study suggests that sameness, in terms of play therapy practice, cannot be taken as given. Closer analysis of a larger data set might identify subgroups of BAPT play therapists.

The BAPT embraces the Rogerian principle of person- or child-centredness which encompasses the idea that therapy is non-directive. This is a philosophical position as well as a practical approach to working with children. It emphasises mutuality of the relationship (Rogers, 1990). An analysis of the qualitative data from the questionnaires revealed quite a variation in both who play therapists worked with as well as the approaches they took in their work. It was interesting to review where play therapists were working, and it was apparent that many of them worked in specialist services, such as hospices, or with non-verbal children or with services for children and families who had witnessed domestic violence. Respondents noted that because of their client base, their approach had been modified. It would be interesting to interrogate this further. Was it on the basis of evidence-based practice that such amendments were made, or was it, at least in part, a reflection of the demands of the service? In times of economic challenges, it is important to extrapolate whose agenda is being served. It is a mistake to structure play therapy according to the measures needed to evidence outputs; we should not fall into the trap whereby "practise becomes shaped by the tools of measurement" (Lowenthal, 2011) or by financial constraints.

Therapists as well as researchers need to be mindful of the reality of power relationships when working with children, both the adult–child relationship but also the institutional power that is imposed by schools, hospitals and to some extent families in which children live and settings where play therapists practise. These power differentials also have the potential to influence therapy, for example with time constraints being imposed and the need for accurate and timely *assessment*, as for example in a safeguarding case, as opposed to *therapy*. These constraints were evidenced by some of the responses from play therapists in the study who needed to 'fit' their approach to the requirements of the referring organisation or individual.

Some respondents, for example, those who work with children that have experienced trauma, acknowledged additional influences to their ways of working with children. These include taking a more directive and proactive approach to child therapy. How they have integrated such models into their way of working is unclear, and whether they have incorporated such practices in an evidence-based way in play therapy is uncertain. As long as the theoretical and philosophical core of play therapy, as it is practised by BAPT members, remains ambiguous, eclecticism rather than a coherent empirically based approach can prevail.

There were some aspects of the CPQ that respondents felt did not adequately reflect play therapy. For example, respondents highlighted how they use the metaphor of the child's play and enter into play through the metaphor without interpreting back to the child. This demonstrates empathic recognition and responsiveness to the child's affects, enabling them to feel known and understood (Barish, 2004). Play therapists do not rely on the verbal communications of the child, nor do they interpret their play; rather, they enter into the child's world of playing by playing with them. The use of the metaphor, symbolic distance and engaging with the child on his terms in his arena is perhaps a unique strength of play therapy. It sets it apart from other therapies, and respondents were concerned that this uniqueness was inadequately accounted for in the CPQ.

Midgley (2012, personal correspondence) identifies item 38 "Therapist and child demonstrate a shared vocabulary or understanding when referring to events or feelings" and suggests that this would be about "things like the therapist taking up a metaphor introduced by the child and further developing it". By making comparisons to other therapeutic interventions, features such as use of metaphor, so prevalent in a play therapist's way of working and central to arts therapies more generally, will become more firmly established as therapeutic and recognised across modalities.

Playfulness is understood to be important in therapeutic engagement as a way of facilitating the child's expression of affect. It is in the context of enthusiastic and playful engagement that we are able to most successfully challenge or 'nudge' children (Fonagy and Target, 1998). One respondent noted the lack of 'playfulness' in the questionnaire although acknowledged that this could be covered by item 74 "Humour is used". Apart from item 74, playfulness is implicit in other items; for example, item 13 states "child is animated or excited", and item 71, "child engages in make believe play", amongst others. It is in the 'interaction structures', the constellations of different items of the therapist and child, and the relationship interactions that qualities such as humour can be identified and evaluated for how characteristic they are within sessions and over time.

Some of the respondents thought that the instrument was too long and could be made more 'user friendly' by being shorter and more focussed on play. The CPQ, because of its design as a Q-sort, cannot be shortened. It operates as a whole, with each item being related to the other 99. Each item is force-sorted into the Q set pattern (Figure 7.2) in relation to the other 99. Schneider uses the analogy of a spider's web to illuminate understanding. Another respondent felt that as a quantitative instrument, it could not be comprehensive enough. Schneider (2004) does not purport to have created an all-inclusive research instrument. Rather the measure "provides a language and rating procedure for describing therapist–child interaction in clinically relevant terms in a form suitable for quantitative comparison and analysis" (Kennedy and Midgely, 2007: 39). It is a very different and tangential approach to session analysis for many play therapists. As well as developing a prototype for play therapy, the CPQ can be used to illuminate the process of a session and plot change over a course of treatment. As such it can be used for further research and analysis of practice as well as the supervision of trainees.

The primary purpose of the CPQ-set is to describe the process of a therapy session with a child. It is designed to be appropriate for use across theoretical orientations, to describe single sessions or sessions over time. It addresses the attitudes and behaviours of the child, the attitudes and behaviours of the therapist and the interactions or 'climate' between them (Anna Freud Centre, 2011). The items are "behaviourally anchored" in as much as they are designed to be independent of theoretical orientations (Schneider et al., 2010: 95). Unlike in my study, which required respondents to rate the items using a Likert scale, the CPQ is used as a Q-sort.

Applications of the CPQ

The CPQ offers numerous possibilities for research as an instrument that can effectively and accurately describe the course of therapy in a quantitative way.

The CPQ instrument lends itself to statistical analyses. A factor analysis of 100 Q-sort items can be conducted with a minimum of 50 sessions. Factors can then be used to describe therapy across sessions with a particular client of a group of children, perhaps with a shared presenting issue. Research questions can be moved from 'which therapy works?' to 'how does therapy work?' (Goodman, 2010b).

The CPQ can be used with outcome measures for single cases (Goodman et al., 2015) and multiple case studies, especially where a prototype has been established. It can also be used to describe a case study for which a complementary qualitative methodology such as grounded theory (Charmaz, 2006) or play behaviours and themes is used to broaden the scope of analysis.

The CPQ can be used for practice analysis, as it provides a framework to identify changes and variations in child, therapist and interactions and formulate an analysis. The CPQ has been used successfully in therapies in which a prototype is more developed and in common usage, such as in psychodynamic psychotherapy with children. It provides an objective assessment of the supervisee's knowledge base of technique, the appropriateness of their typical interventions given the presentation of the child and the improvements demonstrated by the supervisee over time. Goodman describes the use of the CPQ in this way as uncovering "previously hidden aspects of the psychotherapy process and mak[ing] them available for discussion" (2010a: 105) thereby increasing clinical understanding.

Summary

There is limited research that pertains to play therapy and particularly play therapy as it is practised in the UK. Without the existence of a strong tradition in research, there is the opportunity to use new and innovative ways to research play therapy. It is paramount that when choosing a research approach it should be one that is relevant to and representative of play therapy practice. The choice is not merely about quantitative versus qualitative, the process or the outcome, but rather about how we can garner something of the unique essence of play therapy and hold it up for analysis and critique. There is a challenge to all expressive arts psychotherapies of producing words to explain creative expression. This is the very kernel of what therapy is about: putting into words some of the emotions played out, to think about feelings, to make 'sense'.

Play therapy does not, in this country, have an established research base. This works to the detriment of both the profession in its attempt to gain greater credibility and researchers trying to attract interest, funding and involvement in their work. However, the potential for collaboration across therapeutic approaches and internationally is growing exponentially in this digital age.

The purpose of the study described in this chapter was to establish whether a quantitative instrument, such as the CPQ using 100 qualitative items, would be appropriate to both describe and analyse play therapy. Part of this study was to develop a prototype for play therapy. Sufficient play therapists responded to produce a CPQ-set prototype for play therapy as it is practised by BAPT–registered play therapists in the UK. This can now be used both to compare and contrast with alternative prototypes but also has value in comparing to actual play therapy sessions to establish how the prototype is borne out in practice. The CPQ-sort allows us to paint a portrait of the therapeutic process using a predetermined palette of colours. It is not perfect, but it is able to offer a 'likeness'. Respondents were largely supportive of the instrument. The reservations of respondents, including the lack of perceived explicit acknowledgment of symbolism and metaphor used within the therapeutic relationship, have been communicated back to Celeste Schneider, who developed the instrument, for her information. No instrument can claim to describe all the processes within therapy, all the nuances of the therapeutic relationship between child and therapist and the totality of the rich world of play. Nevertheless, I believe in an open-mindedness to research as described by Brenda Meldrum when she urges play therapists to "resist a kind or preciousness that pretends that therapeutic work is a magical mystery tour, unavailable for examination, monitoring and evaluation" (Meldrum, 2007: 177). The Child Psychotherapy Q-Set offers a validated measure of process that has credence across therapeutic modalities and is a way of quantifying the therapeutic encounter in a tangible way. The CPQ goes beyond a mere description of themes or activities within a session and provides a way to identify elements of the therapeutic process that promote change. As such it offers a way of integrating research and practice for the advancement of both.

We need to relinquish the idea of a perfect evaluation tool for play therapy; it is a self-defeating idea. The unique strength of play therapy to tap into the world of a child in the 'language' of the child, through play, is often overlooked in research. Play therapists have an extraordinary opportunity to observe and understand children's behaviours, feelings, communications and relationships. We need to recognise play therapy research for what it is: merely the pursuit of knowledge to better inform practice and understand the lives of the children we have the opportunity to work with. Yet it does require a dynamic and sustained commitment to using different approaches.

Final thoughts

There is no one way of undertaking research, but a range of approaches, qualitative and quantitative, applied with rigor and patience, is required to explicate the value of play therapy and to distil play therapy as a distinct therapeutic modality. Research is essential if play therapy is to be recognised as a valid therapeutic intervention and needs to focus on not only *whether* play therapy 'works' but also *how* it works and for *whom*. The unique strength of play therapy to tap into the world of a child in the 'language' of the child, through play, is often overlooked in research. Play therapists are in a privileged position to develop innovative methodologies. To do this, play therapy practitioners must be not only fluent in the language of play and child behaviour but also confident in the language of research. They will then be best placed to translate and bring their understanding of the experiences of children to a wider audience, including clinicians from other modalities. The value of systematically examining the nature of play therapy is not only pertinent to research but also as a way of understanding, developing and improving practice.

Notes

1 It should be noted that play therapy is being used increasingly with adults (see Schaefer, 2002).
2 For ease of reading, 'she' will be used to denote the therapist and 'he' the child throughout the chapter.
3 For a fuller discussion of the use of the prototype to explore the play therapy processes and mentalisation, see Goodman, Reed & Athey-Lloyd, 2015.

References

Achenbach, T. (1991) *Manual for Child Behaviour Checklist/ 4–18 and 1991 Profile.* Burlington: University of Vermont.

Alderson, P. & Morrow, V. (2011) *The Ethics of Research with Children and Young People: A Practical Handbook.* London: Sage.

Anna Freud Centre (2011) *The Psychotherapy Q-Sort with Children and Adolescents.* Available at www.annafreud.org/courses.php/34/the-psychotherapy-q-sort-with-children-and-adolescents (accessed: 17/12/11).

Axline, V. (1964) *Dibs: In Search of Self.* London & New York: Penguin Books.

Baggerley, J. & Bratton, S. (2010) Building a Firm Foundation in Play Therapy Research: Response to Phillips (2010). *International Journal of Play Therapy* Vol 19 (1), 26–38.

Bambery, M., Porcerelli, J. & Ablon, J. S. (2007) Measuring Psychotherapy Process with the Adolescent Psychotherapy Q-Set (APQ): Development and Applications for Training. *Psychotherapy, Theory, Research, Practice, Training* Vol 44 (4), 405–422.

Barham, M. (2003) Practitioner Based Research: Paradigm or Paradox? *Dramatherapy* Vol 25 (2), 4–7.

Barish, K. (2004) What Is Therapeutic in Child Therapy? *Psychoanalytic Psychology* Vol 21 (3), 385–401.

Bratton, S. & Ray, D. (2000) What Research Shows Us about Play Therapy. *International Journal of Play Therapy* Vol 9 (1), 47–88.

Bratton, S., Ray, T., Rhine, T. & Jones, L. (2005) The Efficacy of Play Therapy with Children: A Meta-Analytic Review of Treatment Outcomes. *Professional Psychology, Research and Practice* Vol 36 (4), 376–390.

British Association of Play Therapists. (2015) Available at www.bapt.info/ (accessed 7/10/15).

Carroll, J. (2005) Children Talk about Play Therapy. In: Schaefer, C., McCormick, J. & Ohnogi, A. (eds.) (2005) *International Handbook of Play Therapy: Advances in Assessment, Theory, Research and Practice* (pp. 197–226). New York: Jason Aronson.

Charmaz, K. (2006) *Constructing Grounded theory: A Practical Guide Through Qualitative Analysis.* London, Thousand Oaks, New Delhi: Sage Publications.

Cochran, N., Nordling, W. & Cochran, J. (2010) *Child-Centered Play Therapy: A Practical Guide to Developing Therapeutic Relationships with Children.* Hoboken, NJ: John Wiley & Sons, Inc.

Crenshaw, D. & Kenney-Noziska, S. (2014) Therapeutic Presence in Play Therapy. *International Journal of Play Therapy* Vol 23 (1), Jan 2014, 31–43.

Daniel-McKeigue, C. (2006) Playing in the Field of Research: Creating a Bespoke Methodology to Investigate Play Therapy Practice. *British Journal of Play Therapy* Vol 2, 24–36.

Elliot, R. (2012) Qualitative Methods for Studying Psychotherapy Changes Processes. In: Harper, D. & Thompson, A. (2012) *Qualitative Research Methods in Mental Health and Psychotherapy: A Guide for Students and Practitioners* (pp. 69–81). Chichester: Wiley-Blackwell

Fonagy, P. & Target, M. (1998) Mentalisation and the Changing Aims of Child Psychoanalysis. *Psychoanalytic Dialogues* Vol 8, 87–114.

Fonagy, P., Target, M., Cottrell, D., Phillips, J. & Kurtz, Z. (2002) *What Works for Whom? A Critical Review of Treatments for Children and Adolescents.* New York & London: Guilford Publications.

Frankel, J. (1998) The Play's the Thing: How the Essential Processes of Therapy Are Seen Most Clearly in Child Therapy. *Psychoanalytic Dialogues* Vol 8, 149–182.

Glazer, H. & Stein, D. (2010) Qualitative Research and Its Role in Play Therapy Research. *International Journal of Play Therapy* Vol 19 (1), 54–61.

Goodman, G. (2010a) *Transforming the Internal World and Attachment, Volume One: Theoretical and Empirical Perspectives.* New York: Toronto: Plymouth: Jason Aronson.

Goodman, G. (2010b) *Transforming the Internal World and Attachment, Volume Two: Clinical Applications.* New York: Toronto: Plymouth: Jason Aronson.

Goodman, G., Reed, P. & Athey-Lloyd, L. (2015) Mentalization and Play Therapy Processes between Two Therapists and a Child with Asperger's Disorder. *International Journal of Play Therapy* Vol 24 (1), 13–29.

Goodman, R. (1997) The Strengths and Difficulties Questionnaire: A Research Note. *Journal of Child Psychology and Psychiatry* Vol 38 (5), 581–586.

Harvey, S. (2011) Pivotal Moments of Change in Expressive Therapy with Children. *British Journal of Play Therapy* Vol 7, 74–85.

Joffe, H. (2012) Thematic Analysis. In: Harper, D. & Thompson, A. (eds.) (2012) *Qualitative Research Methods in Mental Health and Psychotherapy: A Guide for Students and Practitioners* (pp. 209–223). Chichester: Wiley-Blackwell.

Josefi, O. & Ryan, V. (2004) Non-Directive Play Therapy for Young Children with Autism: A Case Study. *Clinical Child Psychology and Psychiatry* Vol 9, 533–551.

Kennedy, E. & Midgley, N. (2007) *Process and Outcome Research in Child, Adolescent and Parent–Infant Psychotherapy: A Thematic Review*. London: NHS.

Landreth, G. (2002) *The Art of the Relationship*, 2nd Edn. New York & London: Routledge.

Lowenthal, D. (2011) *Psychotherapy without Foundations*. Conference Anna Freud Centre, London, 29 October, 2011.

McLaughlin, C., Holliday, C., Clarke, B. & Ilie, S. (2013) *Research on Counselling and Psychotherapy with Children and Young People: A Systematic Scoping Review of the Evidence for Its Effectiveness from 2003–2011*. Lutterworth: British Association of Counselling and Psychotherapy.

McLeod, J. (2001) *Qualitative Research in Counselling and Psychotherapy*. London: Sage.

Meldrum, B. (2007) Research in the Arts Therapies. In: Cattanach, A. (ed) (2008) *Process in the Arts Therapies* (pp. 179–190). London & Philadelphia: Jessica Kingsley Publishers.

Midgley, N. (2012) Email to Paula Reed, 16 February 2012.

Phillips, R. (1985) Whistling in the Dark? A Review of Play Therapy Research. *Psychotherapy* Vol 22 (4), 752–760.

Phillips, R. (2010) How Firm Is Our Foundation? Current Play Therapy Research. *International Journal of Play Therapy* Vol 9 (1), 13–25.

Ray, D. (2011) *Advanced Play Therapy: Essential Conditions, Knowledge and Skills for Child Practice*. New York & Hove: Routledge.

Ray, D. & Schottelkorb, A. (2010) Single-Case Design: A Primer for Play Therapists. *International Journal of Play Therapy* Vol 19 (1), 39–53.

Reddy, L., Files-Hall, T. & Schaefer, C. (2005) *Empirically Based Play Interventions for Children*. Washington, DC: American Psychological Association.

Reed, P. (2012) *Painting by Numbers: An Exploration of the Relevance and Applicability of the Child Psychotherapy Q-Set to Play Therapy Research and Practice* (Unpublished master's dissertation). Dept. of Psychology, University of Roehampton, England.

Rogers, C. (1990) *The Carl Rogers Reader*. London: Constable.

Ryan, V. & Edge, A. (2012) The Role of Play Themes in Non-Directive Play Therapy. *Clinical Child Psychology and Psychiatry* Vol 17 (3), 354–369.

Ryan, V. & Needham, C. (2001) Non-Directive Play Therapy with Children Experiencing Psychic Trauma. *Clinical Child Psychology and Psychiatry* Vol 6, 437–453.

Ryan, V. & Wilson, K. (2000) *Case Studies in Non-Directive Play Therapy*. London & Philadelphia: Jessica Kingsley Publishers Ltd.

Schaefer, C. (ed.) (2002) *Play Therapy with Adults*. Hoboken, NJ: John Wiley & Sons Inc.

Schneider, C. *(2012) The Development and First Trial Application of the Child Psychotherapy Q-set.* Web publication of the International Psychoanalytic Association. Available at www.ipa.world/images/ResearchPapers/109438schneider.pdf (accessed 2/10/15).

Schneider, C. (2011) *Process Research in Play Therapy.* Email sent to Reed, P. (sent 5/09/11).

Schneider, C. & Jones, E. (2004) *Child Psychotherapy Q-Set: Coding Manual.* Available at myweb.cwpost.liu.edu/ggoodman/CPQMANUALFINAL.pdf (accessed: 17/12/11).

Schneider, C., Midgley, N. & Duncan, A. (2010) A Motion Portrait of a Psychodynamic Treatment of an 11-Year-Old Girl: Exploring Interrelations of Psychotherapy Process and Outcome Using the Child Psychotherapy Q-Set. *Journal of Infant, Child, and Adolescent Psychotherapy* Vol 9 (2), 94–107.

Schneider, C., Pruetzel-Thomas, A. & Midgley, N. (2009) Discovering New Ways of Seeing and Speaking about the Psychotherapy Process: The Child Psychotherapy Q-Set. In: Midgley, N., Anderson, J., Grainger, E., Nesic-Vuckovic, T. & Urwin, C. (eds) *Child Psychotherapy and Research: New Approaches, Emerging Findings* (pp. 72–84). London & New York: Routledge.

Snow, M., Wolff, L., Hudspeth, E. & Etheridge, L. (2009) The Practitioner as Researcher: Qualitative Case Studies in Play Therapy. *International Journal of Play Therapy* Vol 18 (4), 240–250.

Urquiza, A. (2010) The Future of Play Therapy: Elevating Credibility through Play Therapy Research. *International Journal of Play Therapy* Vol 19 (1), 4–12.

Van Fleet, R., Sywulak, A. & Sniscak, C. (2010) *Child-Centered Play Therapy.* New York & London: The Guilford Press.

Chapter 8

The role of the process group within a play therapy training programme

A conversation

Elise Cuschieri and David Le Vay

Introduction

The Process Group, within the context of the University of Roehampton MA Play Therapy programme, provides play therapy trainees with an opportunity to experience a boundaried, therapeutic process within an educational framework. It allows trainees the opportunity to reflect upon themselves in relation to others, to explore past and present patterns of relating and to experiment with new ways of being as well as the space to process the developmental experience of their learning. Alongside the acquisition of knew knowledge and skill, the development of self-awareness and personal insight (reflexive learning) is, we would argue, the most core, fundamental aspect of the trainee therapist's learning experience. Although training to become play therapists, essentially a dyadic relationship, we learn about ourselves in the context of the group: the family group, the work group, the play group. The trainee's learning takes place within the context of their student peer group, in this sense as much a group learning process as an individual one, and the opportunity to reflect upon the meaning of this group learning experience is an integral part of the trainee's process.

The Process Group then has, for many years, been seen as a cornerstone of Roehampton's play therapy training. Why this is so perhaps requires some examination. The structure and facilitation of the group have also raised many questions and challenges around how it fits within the context of the overall training programme. To what extent does or should it be placed within or without the programme? How can it/should it be best facilitated? What are the tensions around facilitation and the relative losses and gains of programme lecturers being involved in this process? How do the trainees manage the tensions around being 'in' and 'out' of the group, and how does this impact the overall group process?

Within this chapter, we aim to address some of these questions and to explore the varied processes and dynamics of the Process Group as well as the often recurrent themes that emerge. In terms of our own process, as co-editors of this book and co-authors of this chapter (and both facilitators of Process Groups), we were mindful as to how this task could best be achieved. Our experience of co-authored chapters is that they are invariably problematic, often resulting in individually written sub-sections that belie the notion of an integrated process. So in the spirit of co-construction, we have decided to embark upon a narrative conversation – for the two of us to engage in a dialogue about our own experience as Process Group facilitators and some of the challenges we have encountered along the way.

But before going any further, it may be helpful to clarify our terms of reference. First, whilst clearly being therapeutic, the Process Group is not a therapy group. The distinction lies within the explicit pedagogic context of the group and the inherently stated aims and objectives that are linked to the trainees' learning outcomes, within the overall context of the play therapy programme. A therapy group, we would suggest, will have a different set of aims and objectives, dependent upon the nature of the group, and although there are clearly areas of overlap the distinction is important. That said, the given areas of overlap (between therapy and education) are also a feature of the overall complexity of the Process Group experience, which will be addressed later in this discussion.

The term *Process Group* is used as it exists within the Arts and Play Therapies programmes at the University of Roehampton. Other interchangeable terms are variably used to describe groups of this nature that sit within the context of therapy training programmes, for example, *training group* or *experiential training group*. For the purposes of this discussion, the term *Process Group* will be used throughout.

Literature review

Prior to exploring our own experience as group facilitators, we felt it would be helpful to place the Process Group within something of a theoretical context, to look at how an understanding of relevant theory provides a containing 'edge' to the overall experience, or what are the theoretical foundations of the Process Group and how does this understanding contribute to the notion of a 'held' group process. The literature on Process Groups and their like within therapy training programmes is sparse and, within the arts therapies, even more so. Within play therapy the literature it is non-existent, a fact that has provided further impetus to this chapter. If the Process Group is, as we would propose, an integral part of the play therapy trainee's learning, then it is important that we begin to take some steps towards an understanding of how and why this is so.

Experiential groups can be understood through a variety of conceptual frameworks. Looking through an analytical lens, Winnicott's (1953) concept of 'holding' is of relevance, the notion of emotional and psychological development – and the transitional state between dependence and independence – being applicable to the group process. Drawing a parallel between the group process and that of maternal holding, Winnicott (1990) viewed the developmentally 'immature group' as simply a collection of separate parts requiring a need to be held together by a containing and supportive agency. Prior to integration, Winnicott suggests

there exists "only a primitive pre-group formation, in which unintegrated elements are held together by an environment from which they are not yet differ-
entiated. The environment is the holding mother" (1990: 193). In this sense, the
containing, symbolic cradling of the parental facilitator is a seductive metaphor,
and this clearly raises questions about the role of the facilitator as he or she straddles the divide between the therapeutic and educational objectives (and needs) of
the group.

Jung's concept of the transformative process (1968) is also pertinent: the cir-
cular formation of the group is evocative of the alchemical vessel, sealed in the
context of a closed group. The process of change, both on an individual and collective basis, is of course a fundamental task of the group and can carry powerful
implications for both loss and gain. Reminiscent of Winnicott, this process can
involve aspects of both integration and separation, a tension between the needs of
the group and the individual, and perhaps carries echoes of Jung's work around
transformation and psychic integration.

As stated, the distinction between a therapy group and an educational on is
important – and complex. As Noack (2001) suggests, these groups consist of individuals who are not coming specifically for help with personal problems but are
seeking to become professional therapists in their own right. It could be suggested,
then, that the primary focus of the Process Group is not that of personal change
in the individual, as in a therapy group, but more one of professional development
through an experience of group dynamics and personal insight in relation to the
self and other. But of course as Noack says, "individuals in a professional training
programme are expected to change as well . . . to change into competent and confident professionals who are able to initiate and facilitate change in their clientele"
(Noack, 2001: 17). So change is an implicit part of the Process Group, and in this
sense, in the context of a therapeutic training programme, the professional and
personal selves are inexorably intertwined.

Foulkes, in a departure from the more traditional analytical emphasis on the
individual, held the view that it was the group that was of primary significance –
suggesting that "each individual . . . is basically and centrally determined, inevitably, by the world in which he [sic] lives, the community, the group, of which he
forms part" (Foulkes, 1983: 10). Foulkes's view, reminiscent of latter-day social
construction theory (itself an influential contributor to the theoretical model of
play therapy in the UK), stresses the importance of interconnectedness and inter-
relatedness in our experience of the world and the notion that the individual
cannot be separated from the social context which defines him or her. Indeed,
Foulkes believed that to see an individual as a whole, one needs to see the person
against the backdrop of a group. In this sense, it is the very nature of the group
canvas that brings the individual into sharp relief. Rather than competing, Foulkes balances the co-existent elements of the group and the individual and their
respective relationship to each other. As Davis and Greenland suggest, "they are
like two sides of the same coin. The individual is embedded and permeated by
the social . . . interactions need to be framed in this context to be seen" (Davis

and Greenland, 2002: 275). There is a flow, then, between the needs of the individual and the needs of the group, a dynamic interplay between individual and group identity. Sometimes, or perhaps always at one time or another, this inherent tension will lead to moments of conflict that get played out through the group dynamic.

Of course, within the heated metaphor of Jung's aforementioned alchemical vessel, the thermo-dynamics of conflict, change, anxiety, creativity, resistance and so on are all integral constituents of the transformative group process. Within this process, the containing role of the facilitator is a key (if complex) task. Within the context of a university training programme, these complexities are compounded by the often dual role of facilitators, who may well also be members of the programme teaching staff. The notionally conflictual role of facilitator and assessor raises many complex questions around power, authority, confidentiality and neutrality. Whether these dual roles are truly compatible is open to question and raises implications for programme structure.

Bion (1961) suggested that within every group there are in fact two groups – the 'work group' that focuses upon the primary task of the group and the 'basic assumptions' group that is more an expression of the implicit, underlying dynamics that form part of the group dynamic. The three central basic assumptions, as described by Bion, were those of *fight/flight*, *dependency* and *pairing*, and Bion suggested that when the group adopts or acts out one of these basic assumptions, it interferes with the primary task of the work group. The three basic assumptions, as seen through Bion's analytical lens, are expressions of the groups need for protection, preservation or indeed sexual union (perhaps in the oedipal sense), but whatever we might think about this, recognised within this theoretical perspective is the notion that unconscious or tacit dynamics will invariably have a significant impact upon the group process, or perhaps one could say *is* the group process. One may think of these factors as resistance or perhaps a defence against anxiety, and clearly, while recognising again that Process Groups are not (explicitly) therapy groups, these dynamics are likely to play a significant part in the group's life. That said, establishing precisely the nature of the group's primary task is an interesting question. The non-directive nature of the Process Group reflects the non-directive nature of child-centred play therapy, and in our experience, much of the Process Group's early preoccupation is around the very nature of the group's purpose and the tension between needing to be led and the perceived absence of structure.

Yalom (1970) also contributed greatly to an understanding of group psychotherapy, for example his studies around group cohesiveness, transference and the identification of a number of 'therapeutic factors' or themes drawn from research that looked at how group members experienced the process of group psychotherapy. Again, whilst the context of Yalom's work is that of group psychotherapy, there are clearly elements that can be applied more generally to the dynamics of other group settings, including the Process Group. His writings on transference and transparency are perhaps of particular note in the context of the powerful unconscious dynamics that can get played out within the group. In relation to the role of the group facilitator, Yalom suggests

> the therapist's arrival not only reminds the group of its task but also evokes early constellations of feelings in each member about the adult, the teacher, the evaluator. Without you the group can frolic; your presence is experienced as a stern reminder of the responsibilities of adulthood.
>
> (Yalom, 1970: 203)

This, as suggested earlier, is evocative of both the complexity of the facilitation role and of trainee play therapists whose learning experience oscillates between the personal, the educational and the professional.

Rogers (1970) was also a key, influential figure in the development of group theory – namely the encounter or training group. From a humanistic, person-centred perspective, Rogers held the view that the 'encounter group' enabled people to regain or restore a sense of trust and acceptance of their own feelings through the unconditional positive regard of the group facilitator. In this sense, as the containing security and safety of the group became more established, members were able to let go of their personal defences and façades and encounter each other from a position of authenticity. Again, this has relevance for the Process Group particularly as the students own training in child-centred play therapy is rooted in the principles of Rogerian person-centred theory.

Elise Cuschieri and David Le Vay: A conversation

EC

I'm aware of wanting some kind of structure for what we are about to attempt, that embarking on this without knowing where it is going, what's going to emerge or how, creates anxiety within me. Logically I know that if it's going to be of any use, then we need to let it evolve organically, and yet that feels scary. Which led me to thinking about the groups we facilitate, and I was struck by how both of them, in different ways, have recently found ways to put structure into what is largely an unstructured and non-directive process. I guess it made me think about Bion and the notion of the work group, of the group's task and how that develops. I've been thinking back on the various groups we've facilitated and wondered whether that is always part of the process.

DL

Yes, it is interesting how our own process of engaging in a conversation of this nature about the Process Group raises similar tensions around the relative presence or absence of structure, as you say a reflection of the group process itself.

A case of where and how to begin . . . and not knowing where it may lead us. Of course, the unstructured nature of the group also reflects the process of child-centred play therapy and the uncertainty about whether to lead or be led (and the anxiety this can create in both child and therapist). So much of the group process, certainly in the early stages (and to some extent throughout the group's life), seems to be about managing the anxiety provoked by the absence of structure, and, like you say, it is interesting how both our groups are finding ways to manage this at the moment. Again, thinking about the parallels with play therapy, this is about responsibility being returned to the group. The notion of Bion's work group and the group task is interesting. I think the central challenge of the group in the early stages is grappling with the very question of 'what exactly is our task?' As facilitator, I feel this intensely at times as the group looks for direction.

EC

Yes, the group often looks to us, as facilitators, for direction, and *our* task, as I understand it, is to gently return the direction of that search back to the group, to enable them to discover ways in which they can embody the task of the Process Group. And, of course, although there are similar processes, each group is unique, so as facilitators, our experience mirrors that of the play therapist embarking on a new piece of work with a child, of also 'not knowing', and needing to tolerate uncertainty and anxiety that is around, especially initially. I am always struck by just how much the process of the group parallels or mirrors the play therapy process. And it is interesting when the group members start to make those connections themselves. I find that often happens in the second term when students go out on placement for the first time. It is usually then that there are some links with being able to tolerate 'not knowing', with the role of silence and with the notion of boundaries and containment. I expect these are all themes that will emerge during the course of our conversation, but thinking about the latter two themes, boundaries and containment, makes me reflect on Winnicott and the concept of 'holding'. The transition between dependence and independence seems especially pertinent when I think back to what you said earlier about the group looking to the facilitator for direction.

DL

It's interesting, just as we are talking about the group's uncertainty about their collective, shared task, I realise that I often find myself sitting with the group pondering that very same question – what exactly is *my* task as facilitator? I sometimes find myself questioning my own role just as the group questions theirs – there are so many complex parallel processes at play. In fact, I believe I am clear about my task, but in the face of the group's anxiety (or uncertainty) I am sometimes aware of a sense of being pulled out of role; perhaps a pressure to become more directive or a felt tension between my role of group facilitator and my role as programme lecturer. But perhaps we will return to that? But I think the relationship or transition between dependence and independence – autonomy – is such an intrinsic part of the group's process. I agree with your reference to Winnicott; it makes me think about his writings on the 'capacity to play alone', which in fact is about playing alone in the presence of another (the maternal presence). Independence emerges out of a sense of feeling contained . . . attachment and separation? I am a little worried here about infantilising the group ,and this is not my intention; it is just that the parallels are so strong, and child development lies at the heart of the play therapy training. In fact, one thing I am always struck by, with successive groups, is the very strong connection between the student's experience of their infant observations and the material that gets brought into the group – they seem so interlinked. Have you experienced this?

EC

Yes, in different ways, I would say. Sometimes explicitly, so when students think about the process of observation they are engaged in and make links to their own childhoods or their experiences of children; but also in more unconscious ways, I think, which seems to lie at the heart of what you were alluding to in terms of the process of independence. It seems to link in to the individual and the group's process of *identity formation*; I think it is a parallel process with some obvious links. Part of it, as I see it, is the process in which students begin to take on, as it were, a new identity as they engage more fully in the training, in the process of becoming, in reconstructing their *self*. I often feel this mirrors the process they observe in infant observation, of the emerging 'identity' of the infant. But the other dimension, or perhaps alongside this, is the experience of the individual and the group; how does one support and enhance the growth and development of the other?

DL

The infant observation is clearly a very powerful experience for students, and this makes me realise what a critical, integral element of the course structure it is. Like you say about the connections that students are able to make in the second term as they go out on placement, I think there is a sense that the various modules of the programme, whilst initially being experienced as somewhat disparate, do start to feel more integrated as the course progresses . . . the pieces falling together, you might say. The Process Group seems to be a place where much of this reflecting and integrating takes place – which takes us back to Winnicott and Bion and the notion of 'maternal reverie'. In this sense the group is in many ways a transitional space. On a practical note, I think it is a good thing that they take place at the end of the teaching week as the students move between one space and another.

But I think you are right, if this is what you were meaning, that there is a tension between the needs of the group and the needs of the individual, or perhaps I should say a relationship between the two. . .a kind of flowing back and forth. Staying for a moment with our parallel metaphor of infant observation, this is perhaps something about merging and individuation. How does someone become a part of the group whilst also holding on to a sense of their own identity? This is reminiscent of Foulkes, who as far as I understand viewed the individual and the group more as a both/and rather than an either/or – his view being that the individual is essentially defined *by* the group. This has been a strong theme in my group recently. But I am very struck by the idea of the emerging student identity (and group identity) and the connections this has with the experience of infant observation. There is something very powerful about that. . .the idea of seeing oneself reflected in the observed child.

EC

I think earlier I was reflecting on the notion of the trainee's emerging self as thera-pist and how that mirrors the *process* of infant observation, but I like the idea of the observed infant somehow being a reflection of the student's new identity as play therapist, if that is what you meant . . . But I'd also like to pick up on your point about merging and individuation.

The idea of the individual and the group, and the relationship and tension between the two, seems to be at the heart of Process Group. I am always struck by how this gets played out, or expressed, in each group. Issues linked to time and space, how individual needs can be met, how one can carve out a space, a role within the group, all these seem to be tensions individuals hold on to with questions such as is there enough time/space for me, am I occupy-ing too much time, what is my role – to talk, to be silent, to be helpful, often proving to be preoccupying for students, especially at the beginning of the group's life. But inevitably questions about how the group's needs, task and role can be defined, expressed and responded to are also present. This creates a complex weave, and there is a particular tension within the Process Group at Roehampton due to the fact that students find themselves in many different groups on the course– infant observation seminars, clinical supervision, the wider main group. The fact, also, that each group has its own permutation with regard to members adds to the complexity. Recently two students realised that they were together in every group they form part of on the programme. This might be fine most of the time, but I wonder how any tension or conflict might be expressed and in what group space this would surface. It makes me think of Bion's basic assumption group where the unconscious tendency is 'flight'. I wonder whether this is a common challenge for Process Groups that we facilitate.

All of the above coupled with our own roles, as you mentioned above, as facili-tators and also lecturers, creates a challenging process. I am aware that this is an area that I come back to time and again in my reflections on the group – just how far the group can go, given the boundary issues all of the above raises. How safe is Process Group to fully explore the dynamics between individuals, to remain 'on task' when that may lead to conflict that could spill over? These are questions that I feel lie at the heart of what I grapple with regularly whilst sitting with the group. I have come to see them as challenges that bring with them their own opportunity for creativity, but I am aware that they also result in some groups treading carefully, if you like.

DL

You know, as we get further into this conversation I have this strong sense of walking into a deep forest; there are so many complex, interwoven, tangled issues at play and so many different paths we could take. Perhaps it is a fear of getting lost! In fact, I just had flashback from many years ago: of walking into the honeycombed souks of Marrakesh, knowing that I was going to get completely lost but trusting that, one way or another I would find my way out again. I did. . .eventually!

Re the infant observation, yes. . .that was partly what I meant, that is, the student's emerging identity as a play therapist, but I think it was also the idea of observing a child and seeing one's own childhood reflected. I guess it is something about the powerful projective material that this experience of intense observation clearly evokes in the student (this was brought home to me recently when a group member brought in a photograph of herself as a young child). But I am struck – and curious – about the fact that I seem to have become quite preoccupied by the relationship between the Process Group and the infant observation module.

This connects I think with what you were saying about role; to talk, be silent, helpful and so forth. The group is such a potent space (potential space?) for these early, childhood and familial roles to be played out. Again, as Foulkes might suggest, it is the background canvas of the group that brings the individual into sharp relief. This is, in my view, such an important part of the group's task: for the students to gain a level of insight and self-awareness regarding how these powerful, early scripts around role can get played out or re-enacted – particularly in the playroom of course.

I very much agree with what you say about the complex boundary issues that the respective groups have to negotiate. This is a real challenge and does as you say raise questions around safety and containment. It certainly does create a degree of anxiety about how far the group can safely explore. . .to 'play alone', I guess we might say. In fact, the organisational structure of the group does place them in something of a double bind. Flight is a response to this, I think, and the potential for exploring conflict is limited by the potential consequences, for instance, of something spilling over into the wider group. I think there is some learning for us as a department here and the relative pros and cons of the group being facilitated by members of the programme staff.

This does, as you suggest, have real implications for the functioning of the Process Group.

EC

I am interested in your thoughts about the links between Process Group and infant observation. Are you suggesting that the observations somehow aid the individual to be more explicit *in the group* about their childhood memories, roles? That the Process Group becomes a vehicle for the emerging insight into the individual's childhood? I don't know that I have made that link before, but it is an interesting thought and one that I would like to explore further.

I agree with your point about the group's task of increasing self-awareness and insight, and it reminds me of the Johari window. From a practical point of view, I think it can be a helpful tool for students to conceptualise the aims of the Process Group in a more visual manner. But it also makes me think about boundary issues again, particularly with regard to how authority, power and intimacy are played out in the groups. In the early stages of the group, I am often aware of the individual members directing their comments to me, but as the group develops, they start to address each other. It seems to be a process of 'orientation' and, as the group orientates itself away from me, authority, towards an increased intimacy amongst each other. This seems a positive process, and yet I question how much students feel able, and willing, to challenge *our* roles when they have to relate to us both as Process Group facilitators in the first year and then as their lecturers in the second year of the programme. I think this has the potential to curtail the group's exploration of authority and power, and with it, possibly, greater exploration of early scripts and roles that you mentioned.

I have found myself reflecting on this dialogue we are engaged in and wondering whether it is going to prove too circuitous and windy to be of any use to anyone. Your Moroccan souks seem to be a good metaphor for our process! And yet, at the very same moment that I feel maybe we should find another route, I am struck once again by the parallel process of this task with that of the Process Group and with my own feelings and those of the group. Should I 'speak'? How should I respond? What happens if I remain silent? What about my 'voice', my 'space' – is there too much, too little? And, of course, the fact that even though as facilitators of the Process Group and authors of this chapter, we still don't really know what is going to emerge. It's a conundrum . . .

The last point I want to make for today is the issue of what happens in the 'here and now' and how much to work with that. For instance, I sometimes find that discussions remain on a cognitive level, where the group becomes more of a thinking space than a feeling one; I understand this to be a form of avoidance, of shying away from deeper engagement with the process and with each other. My question then is whether to intervene, focus on the 'here and now' and thus bring it back to the group, or to be patient and wait for the process to unfold.

I know there is no definitive answer, as it were, but I wonder if you have any thoughts on this.

DL

Well, to stay with Marrakesh for just a moment longer, I recall that whilst losing myself in the souks and eventually finding my way out again, I found myself in an entirely different place from where I started, which is perhaps the essence of the analogy. It is something about the process of personal change that comes with a developing level of insight and awareness, indeed the process of training to become a therapist. The notion of change has been a strong theme in my group recently, both on an intrinsic level and also in the different way group members feel they are perceived or experienced by close friends and family. There is a sense of the training leaving them feeling fundamentally altered, with all the losses and gains that this entails. It takes us back to the Noack reference at the beginning of this chapter, which acknowledges that whilst personal change may not be an explicit task of the Process Group (as distinct from a therapy group), it is certainly implicit in the process. Interestingly, in the group this week there was a lot of discussion about the idea of getting lost, losing a sense of one's identity – or perhaps personality – and the need to retain some sense of self. This was expressed by one group member as an experience of being deconstructed and reconstructed, and I think there is a point – within this process – that one can be left feeling as if you know nothing.

What I think is so valuable about the group is that it provides a space where these feelings can be expressed, shared and understood. It is a place where the complex feelings that are stirred up by other elements of the course, for example infant observation, can be allowed to coalesce and come together, and much of this does I feel concern reflections on childhood and familial roles. I agree that the Johari window is a good model for conceptualising the tasks of the group, and the power of a group process is that it allows people to experience how they are perceived by others and those parts of themselves that may be more hidden. . .depending upon the group's capacity to take risks perhaps? And this I think connects with your thoughts about power and authority and the group's capacity to challenge – either themselves or us as facilitators. Added to this complexity is the fact that students have to submit a reflective essay of their experience within the group; so there is a degree to which their participation is assessed. This holds real implications re issues of power and authority and the extent to which students can fully open themselves to the process.

Regarding your thoughts on attending to the 'here and now' of the group, this is something that I feel uncertain about at times, in terms of how and when to intervene. I agree that when the group moves into thinking and intellectualising this does feel like a form of avoidance – another form of flight perhaps? I often experience a tension at these moments. . .which possibly links to feelings of collusion in the sense of what it means to do nothing. At times I might just simply express to the group what I am noticing or feeling – to try and be congruent – and at other times I might attempt to bring the focus of the discussion back into the room. . .not always successfully, I should add. The other real tension here is that between anxiety and creativity and the extent to which, being a play therapy Process Group, I should 'encourage' playful, creative methods of group exploration. At times I do find myself becoming more active in this respect by inviting the group to participate in a creative activity, but I am always struck about the group's often-expressed need to 'play' and the boxes of objects, paint, clay and the like that sit, often untouched, in the room. True to the spirit of child-centred play therapy, there are some real directive/non-directive dilemmas here. . .both for the group and certainly for myself.

EC

I have been reflecting on what we have written so far and the various routes we have taken . . . there are certainly many paths in your souk! We seem to be touching on some broad themes and I decided to reflect on the current groups we are facilitating as well as to think back on the groups I have been involved with to date in order to identify recurring themes. I don't know if you would agree but it seems to me that most of what we have articulated so far, in terms of thoughts, observations and also dilemmas, are common to all the groups we have facilitated. Thus I thought it might be useful to name some of them.

The way in which the Process Group mirrors some of the *processes* of child-centred play therapy seems a fundamental theme; and inherent in this are the issues of structure, direction, the non-directive approach and trust in the process. I believe all of this raises interesting questions for both students and for us in terms of how the group is run and the extent to which we as facilitators of a *group* are also role models to a process that is usually carried out on a one-to-one basis in child-centred play therapy. Identity and the process of change seem to be another two interlinked themes; pertinent issues emerge from these, such as how students begin to integrate the impact of the training on their core 'selves' and, as a consequence, how that change can affect the students' roles and relationships with family and friends. The manner in which students begin to recognise and acknowledge early childhood roles and scripts seems another theme, or maybe an extension of the previous one, and here the role of the infant observation module seems particularly pertinent. How this is expressed and explored in the Process Group seems to be a very useful and relevant connection. Another theme that has emerged is our dual role as educators and facilitators, which is challenging, and the dual role that the students have with each other – both as members of an experiential group and as students in the wider group. This thought took me to Yalom, and I remembered reading something in my early days as facilitator which really resonated for me and helped me understand the Process Group *process* in a clearer light. Yalom and Leszcz (2005: 555) state that ". . . it is extremely difficult to lead groups of mental health professionals who will continue to work together throughout their training. The pace is slow; intellectualisation is common; and self-disclosure and risk taking are minimal." I guess this is an inherent challenge for us *and* the students. Our task seems to be to help the students to find ways to embrace this challenge.

What is interestingly *absent* from our discussion so far, or at any rate *mostly* absent, is what happens when the group plays – or doesn't play, as the case may be. You refer to the boxes of toys and such that sit largely untouched during Process Group sessions and this certainly mirrors my experience of the groups I have facilitated. I am struck by this, by the fact that the tendency seems to be to talk about *wanting* to play, about how they *might* play and what they *might* do, and yet few groups do truly engage with the toys and creative materials we provide. I have been wondering about this and thought about the other groups we run, such as the short introductory and Summer School courses. My experience of participants in these groups is that there is a greater willingness to embrace playful activity and, crucially, to be open to its potential impact. The students on our MA programme often seem less playful with the materials we offer, less creative perhaps. I wonder whether this somehow relates to the students' growing awareness of the power of the unconscious, that they become more guarded perhaps about self-disclosure. I wonder whether this is borne out of concern with, and reticence about, the student's own personal and professional sense of competency as a developing therapist. Once again, I think this could be partially due to our dual role and the students' fear of exposure with the risk of negative assessment and judgement from us as staff members.

I have also continued to think about the role that attending to the 'here and now' plays in the Process Group. I do believe the process of gradually and gently helping the group to focus on this aspect is critical but also challenging for the group and for us as facilitators, as you have articulated. I was reminded of Yalom's thoughts about this and the way in which he refers to 'process commentary' being 'taboo social behaviour' (Yalom and Leszcz, 2005: 150). He discusses how alien it is for us as adults to make comments about another's behaviour or presentation, that in everyday interaction, it would be construed as being rude or inappropriate. So, it seems our task in the group is not only to help the group think about what is happening in the moment but also to support them to eschew societal norms and conventions in order to find ways of describing and talking about the process, about what is happening amongst themselves, and between me and the group. My experience is that as students begin working with children on placement, they start to become more aware of the importance of 'noticing', of being sensitive to the minutiae of the present moment. How that then becomes generalised to the group process and how we facilitate that is perhaps another point to chew on . . .

DL

You have very helpfully pulled together the threads of our discussion. It is indeed a complex weave, and as you name some of the emerging themes within our conversation, it does make me acutely aware of the many challenges, dilemmas, obstacles and opportunities that both the students and ourselves have to negotiate during the life of the group. The quote from Yalom about the challenge of working with groups who are training and working together is very pertinent and I think accurately underlines the experiential double bind that students find themselves in. To be truly open, authentic and genuine means to take risks, which could have potentially far-reaching consequences outside of the group. As we were just discussing recently, this is particularly the case with feelings of conflict and anger. These are feelings that as facilitators (and therapists) we would seek to address, explore and name openly, but to do so within the Process Group does feel a real challenge. Certainly, as facilitator, I am at times acutely aware of the inherent risks in naming these feelings and in this sense find myself experiencing the very same double bind as the group members. This has been a strong dynamic within my current group, and as I write this, I am conscious of my felt need to name this dilemma within the group, I guess to try and be as authentic as possible about how I am experiencing the process. I guess this links to the idea of 'noticing' that you talk about and perhaps at times it is less challenging for the group to notice what we, as facilitators, are feeling, than it is to name feelings in the group. Of course, in the absence of expression, feelings of conflict and anger can only be suppressed and played out in less conscious ways, which takes us back to the constant oscillation between positions of fight and flight – and the somewhat dissociative, freeze-like silence perhaps. But also, to take another view, there are possible strengths to how the groups are structured, perhaps in the very intensity of the students learning alongside each other and the capacity to manage boundaries, tolerate uncertainty and learn about the importance of containment. But it is, as Yalom suggests in your earlier quote, a slower process, and this makes me think about how different it would be if the groups could continue throughout both years of the training, rather than just the first.

The issue about play (or the absence of play) within the groups is very interesting, and as you say, the theme of the relationship between anxiety and creativity has been a recurring dynamic, to varying degrees, over time. I think the point you make about the students' developing awareness of the role of the unconscious and their own feelings of competence versus incompetence that get evoked during the course of their training is very true. It is a little ironic perhaps that the students' capacity to play might diminish during the process of their training to become play therapists, but also I wonder if this is a particular feature of the Process Group and not necessarily the case within other areas of the programme. This has some connections with my earlier chapter on the use of self and the study on therapy training I mention by Skovholt and Rønnestad (1992), in which trainees reported that their anxiety around the need for strict adherence to theory stifled their natural sense of humour and playfulness. In fact, I think our discussion about the groups connects with aspects of both the use of self and feelings of incompetence that we have discussed elsewhere in this book. But I think, as you suggest, that the absence of play within the groups is also about the fear of self-disclosure. In fact, one of the students in my group just this week said that she chose not to play or use the materials in the room as it would make her feel too vulnerable. I am aware that as play therapists we talk a lot about the need to tolerate uncertainty and that the much-expressed aspiration of 'trust the process' is something of a well-versed mantra for trainees. But what does this really mean, I wonder? Feelings of incompetence, self-doubt, use of self, issues of culture or gender – all that we have discussed in this book in fact – means that at times it becomes very hard to trust the process. I would suggest that there are times, either as trainees or experienced therapists, that we can't trust the process, and we need the support of theoretical knowledge, personal therapy or clinical supervision to know that what we are doing is good enough. And is 'good enough' always good enough? One needs to trust oneself to be able to trust the process, a state unconscious competence perhaps, and during the course of our writing together I have become acutely aware of the many complex challenges that both trainees and qualified play therapists need to negotiate. Sorry, Elise – I realise I have thrown a lot of things onto the table here but I think these are all part and parcel of what gets played out in the groups.

But the other issue this discussion raises is how the play therapy Process Group sits alongside the Process Groups within the wider arts therapies department. For example, the modalities of art, music, drama or dance movement – what we might think of as adult, sublimed, culturally aesthetic forms of play – perhaps lend themselves more easily to a process of creative expression within a group context. Within a play therapy Process Group this feels less clear. . .how as adults we capture, facilitate and express a sense of playfulness. But this might well be a discussion for another day!

Conclusion

Discussions for another day indeed. As we embarked on our rather free-wheeling conversation around our experience of facilitating the Process Groups we soon realised that we had no clear sense of where it would lead us and how we would draw it to a close. In fact, the conversation continues, as we are sure it will do for some time to come. Like much of this book, perhaps all we have managed to do is ask more questions; but then play therapy and the process of engaging in children's creative, imaginative play is all about curiosity and wondering where the play might lead us. What we have both taken away from this experience is that within and amongst all of the many complex, inherent challenges that both we and the students have to negotiate, the Process Group clearly provides an important and unique space for the students to explore their experience of learning – and what it means to train as a child-centred play therapist.

But we are acutely aware that this is a conversation that we need to explore further and that within this, the voice of the students themselves is central. The other side of this conversation is about the students' experience of the group and their own sense of the part it plays in helping them integrate the various aspects of their learning experience. We can (and have) within our discussion made many assumptions around what we think the meaning of the group might be and how we think students might have experienced it, and these assumptions need checking out, so perhaps this is more a pause than an ending.

References

Bion, W. R. (1961) *Experiences in Groups*. London: Tavistock.
Davies, A. & Greenland, S. (2002) A Group Analytical Look at Experiential Training Groups: How Can Music Earn Its Keep? In: Davies, A. & Richards, E. (eds) *Music Therapy and Group Work: Sound Company* (p. 75). London: Jessica Kingsley.
Foulkes, S. H. (1983) *Introduction to Group Analytic Psychotherapy*. London: Karnac.
Jung, C. G. (1968) *Psychology and Alchemy*. Collected Works of C. G. Jung, Volume 12. Princeton, NJ: Princeton University Press.
Noack, A. (2002) Working with Trainees in Experiential Groups. In: Chesner, A. & Hahn H. (eds) *Creative Advances in Group Work* (pp. 14–39). London: Jessica Kingsley.
Rogers, C. (1970) *On Encounter Groups*. London: HarperCollins.
Skovholt, T. M. & Rønnestad, M. D. (1992) *The Evolving Professional Self: Stages and Themes in Therapists and Counselor Development*. Chichester, UK: Wiley.
Winnicott, D. (1953) Transitional Objects and Transitional Phenomena. *International Journal of Psychoanalysis* Vol 34, 89–97.
Winnicott, D. W. (1990) Group Influences and the Maladjusted Child. In: Winnicott, D., Davis, M. & Winnicott, C. (eds) *Deprivation and Delinquency* (pp. 162–171). London: Routledge.
Yalom, I. D. (1970) *The Theory and Practice of Group Psychotherapy*, 3rd Edn. New York: Basic Books.
Yalom, I. D. & Leszcz, M. (2005) *The Theory and Practice of Group Psychotherapy*, 5th Edn. New York: Basic Books.

Contributor biographies

Elise Cuschieri is a qualified teacher and play therapist and is a senior lecturer at the University of Roehampton, where she teaches on the MA Play Therapy programme. Her interests include the roles of personal therapy and process group in play therapy training as well as the overall experience of therapeutic training for students. Her clinical practice is in a specialist bereavement service, where she works with children and their families pre- and post-bereavement. She is particularly interested in the role of child-centred play therapy with children and young people who have experienced traumatic parental loss. She is also interested in how play therapy can help children, young people and their families who have been affected by parental substance misuse and domestic violence, having worked as a play therapist for many years in this area.

David Le Vay is a qualified and accredited play therapist, dramatherapist and social worker. Since qualifying as a therapist in 1992, he has worked with children who have experienced significant loss, trauma and abuse, as well as with their families and carers. David has particular experience over the last 15 years of working with a service that provides therapeutic support for children and young people with sexually harmful and problematic behaviour. He is also a Senior Lecturer at Roehampton University on their MA Play Therapy programme and an approved BAPT play therapy supervisor.

Natalie Prichard is a qualified play therapist, counsellor and occupational therapist with more than 10 years of experience working with children and families in Australia and the UK. She is currently completing a PhD at the University of Roehampton, London.

Paula Reed trained first as a dancer and then as a nurse. Her PhD explored the meaning of dignity for children in hospital. This experience of doing research with children and trying to understand their worlds led her to train as a play therapist. After qualifying, she worked extensively with children in a pre-bereavement setting. She is a lecturer on the MA Play Therapy programme at the University of Roehampton and works independently as a play therapist and supervisor. She has a special interest in working with children who are affected by physical illness either in themselves or in family members.

Geraldine Thomas is a filial therapist and a child-centred play therapist in private practice. She is a certified filial therapy instructor with the Family Enhancement and Play Therapy Centre, an associate researcher with the Centre for Abuse and Trauma Studies and works as a consultant to Children and Family Services. Her clinical work is informed and guided by attachment theory, and she works with adult attachment style to aid therapeutic progress in children and families. She is also the co-author of *Understanding Adult Attachment Style, Research, Assessment, and Intervention* (Routledge, 2012).

Jan Vance professionally qualified in play therapy at Roehampton University in 2003 after a 30-year career in lecturing, media and management, following her graduation in social science in 1971. For the following 9 years she worked as the play therapist and manager of the play services department at a residential rehabilitation unit for children and adolescents who had sustained sudden and severe acquired brain injury. During this time she provided more than 1,500 hours of direct play therapy to more than 90 children and adolescents.

Index

Note: Italicized page numbers indicate a figure on the corresponding page. Page numbers in bold indicate a table on the corresponding page.